P9-CPX-927

LINCOLN CHRISTIAN UNIVERSITY

PENGUIN CLASSICS

THE SONG OF ROLAND

DOROTHY LEIGH SAYERS was the translator of Dante's *Divine Comedy* for the Penguin Classics. She graduated with first class honours in medieval literature from Somerville College, Oxford, in 1915, having already published two volumes of poetry. Her first novel appeared in 1923 and she later wrote fifteen more crime novels and books of fiction including *The Nine Tailors*, a fascinating novel about campanology. She also wrote religious plays, notably *The Man Born to Be King*. She died in 1957.

LINCOLN CHRISTIAN UNIVERSITY

THE SONG OF ROLAND

*

TRANSLATED BY
Dorothy L. Sayers

PENGUIN BOOKS

PENGUIN BOOKS
Published by the Penguin Group
Penguin Group (USA) Inc., 375 Hudson Street, New York, New York 10014, U.S.A.
Penguin Group (Canada), 90 Eglinton Avenue East, Suite 700, Toronto,
Ontario, Canada M4P 2Y3 (a division of Pearson Penguin Canada Inc.)
Penguin Books Ltd, 80 Strand, London WC2R 0RL, England
Penguin Ireland, 25 St Stephen's Green, Dublin 2, Ireland (a division of Penguin Books L
Penguin Group (Australia), 250 Camberwell Road, Camberwell,
Victoria 3124, Australia (a division of Pearson Australia Group Pty Ltd)
Penguin Books India Pvt Ltd, 11 Community Centre, Panchsheel Park, New Delhi – 110 017,
Penguin Group (NZ), 67 Apollo Drive, Rosedale, North Shore 0632, New Zealand
(a division of Pearson New Zealand Ltd)
Penguin Books (South Africa) (Pty) Ltd, 24 Sturdee Avenue,
Rosebank, Johannesburg 2196, South Africa

Penguin Books Ltd, Registered Offices: 80 Strand, London WC2R 0RL, England

First published 1957

60   59   58   57

Copyright © Executors of Dorothy L. Sayers, 1957
All rights reserved

ISBN 978-0-14-044075-1

Printed in the United States of America
Set in Monotype Bembo

Except in the United States of America, this book is sold subject to the condition
that it shall not, by way of trade or otherwise, be lent, resold, hired out, or otherwise
circulated without the publisher's prior consent in any form of binding or cover other
than that in which it is published and without a similar condition including
this condition being imposed on the subsequent purchaser.

The scanning, uploading and distribution of this book via the Internet or via any
other means without the permission of the publisher is illegal and punishable by law.
Please purchase only authorized electronic editions, and do not participate in or encoura
electronic piracy of copyrighted materials. Your support of the author's rights is appreciat

CONTENTS

124233

INTRODUCTION

I. THE POEM

IN the year 777, a deputation of Saracen princes from Spain came
to the Emperor Charlemagne to request his assistance against cer-
tain enemies of theirs, also of the Moslem faith. Charlemagne, who
was already engaged in a war against the Saxons, nevertheless
accepted their invitation, and, after placing garrisons to fortify
his frontiers, marched into Spain with all his available forces. He
divided his army into two parts, one of which crossed the eastern
Pyrenees in the direction of Gerona; the other, under his own
command, crossed the Basque Pyrenees and was directed upon
Pampeluna. Both cities fell, and the two armies joined forces
before Saragossa, which they besieged without success. A fresh
outbreak of hostilities by the Saxons obliged Charlemagne to
abandon the Spanish expedition. As he was repassing the Pyrenees,
the rear-guard of his army was set upon by a treacherous party of
Basques, who had disposed an ambuscade along the high wooded
sides of the ravine which forms the pass. Taking advantage of the
lie of the land and of the lightness of their armour, they fell upon
the rear-guard, slaughtered them to a man, pillaged the baggage-
train, and dispersed under cover of the falling night. The chronicler
Eginhardt, who recounts this sober piece of history in his *Vita
Caroli*, written about 830, concludes: "In the action were killed
Eggihard the king's seneschal, Anselm count of the palace, and
Roland duke of the Marches of Brittany, together with a great
many more." Another manuscript of the ninth century contains an
epitaph in Latin verse upon the seneschal Eggihard, which furnishes
us with the date of the battle, 15 August 778. The episode is men-
tioned again in 840 by another chronicler, who, after briefly sum-
marising the account given in the *Vita Caroli*, adds that, since the
names of the fallen are already on record, he need not repeat them
in his account.

After this, the tale of Roncevaux appears to go underground for some two hundred years. When it again comes to the surface, it has undergone a transformation which might astonish us if we had not seen much the same thing happen to the tale of the wars of King Arthur. The magic of legend has been at work, and the small historic event has swollen to a vast epic of heroic proportions and strong idealogical significance. Charlemagne, who was 38 at the time of his expedition into Spain, has become a great hieratic figure, 200 years old, the snowy-bearded king, the sacred Emperor, the Champion of Christendom against the Saracens, the war-lord whose conquests extend throughout the civilised world. The expedition itself has become a major episode in the great conflict between Cross and Crescent, and the marauding Basques have been changed and magnified into an enormous army of many thousand Saracens. The names of Eggihardt and Anselm have disappeared from the rear-guard; Roland remains; he is now the Emperor's nephew, the "right hand of his body", the greatest warrior in the world, possessed of supernatural strength and powers and hero of innumerable marvellous exploits; and he is accompanied by his close companion Oliver, and by the other Ten Peers, a chosen band of superlatively valorous knights, the flower of French chivalry. The ambuscade which delivers them up to massacre is still the result of treachery on the Frankish side; but it now derives from a deep-laid plot between the Saracen king Marsilion and Count Ganelon, a noble of France, Roland's own stepfather; and the whole object of the conspiracy is the destruction of Roland himself and the Peers. The establishment of this conspiracy is explained by Ganelon's furious jealousy of his stepson, worked out with a sense of drama, a sense of character, and a psychological plausibility which, in its own kind, may sustain a comparison with the twisted malignancy of Iago. In short, beginning with a historical military disaster of a familiar kind and comparatively small importance, we have somehow in the course of two centuries achieved a masterpiece of epic drama – we have arrived at the *Song of Roland*.

The poem itself as we know it would appear to have achieved its final shape towards the end of the eleventh century. It is not difficult to see why the legend should have taken the form it did, nor why it should have been popular about that time. The Saracen menace to Christendom became formidable about the end of the tenth century, and led to a number of expeditions against the Moors in Spain with a definitely religious motive. At the same time, a whole series of heroic legends and poems were coming into circulation along the various great trade-routes and pilgrim-routes of Europe – legends attached to the names of local heroes, and associated with the important towns and monasteries along each route. The pilgrim-road to the important shrine of St James of Compostella led through the very pass in which Charlemagne's rear-guard had made its disastrous last stand: what more natural than that the travellers should be entertained with a glorified version of the local tragedy? It was also the tenth century that saw the full flowering of the feudal system and the development of the code of chivalry which bound the liegeman in bonds of religious service to his lord and loyalty to his fellow-vassal. And finally, the preaching of the First Crusade set all Christendom on fire with enthusiasm for the Holy War against the followers of Mohammed.

We have little external evidence about the *Song of Roland*. Such as it is, it seems to agree with the internal evidence (of language, feudal customs, arms and accoutrements, names of historical personages anachronistically annexed to the Charlemagne-legend, and scraps of what looks like authentic knowledge of Saracen territories and peoples) in placing the *Chanson de Roland*, as we have it, shortly after the First Crusade. I say, the Chanson as we have it – for the *legend* of Roland must have begun much earlier. Our poet, in beginning his story, takes it for granted that his audience know all about Charlemagne and his Peers, about the friendship of Roland and Oliver, and about Ganelon: like Homer, he is telling a tale which is already in men's hearts and memories. What no scholar has yet succeeded in tracing is the stages by which history transformed itself into legend and legend into epic. Roland, duke of the Marches of Brittany, must have been an important man; but no further historical allusion to him has as yet been traced – why should he have been chosen for this part of epic hero to the exclusion of others who fought and fell with him? How was the story transmitted, and in what form? Ballads? Earlier improvisations of a primitive epic kind? We do not know.[1] We can only fall back on the vague but useful phrase "oral tradition", and refer, if we like, to Sir Maurice Bowra's monumental work, *Heroic Poetry*, which reveals how quickly and how strangely, even at this time in parts of Central Europe, the history of today may become the recited epic of tomorrow. One thing is certain – the extant *Chanson de Roland* is not a chance assembly of popular tales: it is a deliberate and masterly work of art, with a single shaping and constructive brain behind it, marshalling its episodes and its characterisation into an orderly and beautifully balanced whole.

Happily, we may leave scholars to argue about origins: our business is with the poem itself – *the Song of Roland*; just one, the earliest, the most famous, and the greatest, of those Old French epics which are called "Songs of Deeds" – *Chansons de Geste*. It is short, as epics go: only just over four thousand lines; and, though it is undoubtedly great literature, it is not in the least "literary". Its very strength and simplicity, its apparent artlessness, may deceive us into thinking it not only "primitive" (which it is) but also "rude" or "naïve", which it is not. Its design has a noble balance of proportion, and side by side with the straightforward thrust-and-hammer of the battle scenes we find a remarkable psychological sublety in the delineation of character and motive. But all this is left for us to find; the poet is chanting to a large mixed audience which demands a quick-moving story with plenty of action, and he cannot afford the time for long analytical digressions in the manner of a Henry James or a Marcel Proust.

The style of epic is, in fact, rather like the style of drama: the characters enter, speak, and act, with the minimum of stage-setting and of comment by the narrator. From time to time a brief "stage-direction" informs us that this person is "rash" and the other "prudent", that so-and-so is "angry" or "grieved", or has "cunningly considered what he has to say". But for the most part we have to watch and listen and work out for ourselves the motives

1. A page, recently rediscovered, from the Codex Emiliense 39 attests the existence, at or shortly before the date of the *Chanson de Roland*, of a Roland-legend, analogous to, but independent of, the *Chanson* (see *Revista de Filologia Española*, 1953, pp. 1–94).

which prompt the characters and the relationship between them. We are seldom shown their thoughts or told anything about them which is not strictly relevant to the action. Some points are never cleared up. Thus we are never told what is the original cause of the friction between Roland and his stepfather; not until the very end of the poem does Ganelon hint that "Roland had wronged [him] in wealth and in estate", and we are left to guess at the precise nature of the alleged injury. Very likely it was all part of the original legend and already well-known to the audience; or the traditional jealousy between stepparent and stepchild, so familiar in folklore, could be taken for granted. But we do not really need to know these details. The general situation is made sufficiently clear to us in the first words Roland and Ganelon speak. The opening scenes of the poem are indeed a model of what an exposition should be. The first stanza tells us briefly what the military situation is; the scene of Marsilion's council gets the action going and shows us that the Saracens are ready for any treacherous business; the great scene of Charlemagne's council introduces all the chief actors on the Christian side and sketches swiftly and surely the main lines of their characters and the position in which they stand to one another: Charlemagne – at the same time cautious and peremptory; Roland, brave to the point of rashness, provocative, arrogant with the naïve egotism of the epic hero, loyal, self-confident, and open as the day; Oliver, equally brave, but prudent and blunt, and well aware of his friend's weaknesses; Duke Naimon, old and wise in council; Turpin, the fighting archbishop, with his consideration for others and his touch of ironic humour; Ganelon, whose irritable jealousy unchains the whole catastrophe. Ganelon is not a coward, as he proves later on in the poem, and his advice to conclude a peace is backed up by all his colleagues. But it is unfortunate that, after Roland has pointed out that the proposed mission is dangerous and that Marsilion is not to be trusted, he does not at once volunteer to bell the cat himself. He lets others get in first. Charlemagne vetoes their going, and so shows that he too is aware of the danger and doubtful about Marsilion. Then Roland names Ganelon – and coming when it does, and from him, the thing has the air of a challenge. And Charlemagne does not veto Ganelon – infuriating

proof that he values him less than Naimon or Turpin, less than
Roland or any of the Twelve Peers. Ganelon's uneasy vanity
reacts instantly: "This is a plot to get rid of me" – and Roland (who
has quite certainly never had any such idea in his simple mind)
bursts out laughing. That finishes it. Rage and spite and jealousy,
and the indignity of being publicly put to shame, overthrow a
character which is already emotionally unstable. Self-pity devours
him; he sees himself mortally injured and persecuted. He is
obsessed by a passion to get even with Roland at the price of every
consideration of honour and duty, and in total disregard of the
consequences. The twentieth century has found a word for Ganelon:
he is a paranoiac. The eleventh-century poet did not know the
word, but he has faithfully depicted the type.

What is interesting and dramatic in the poet's method is the way
in which the full truth about Ganelon only emerges gradually as
the story proceeds. We are kept in suspense about him. We cannot
at first be certain whether he is a brave man or a coward. When he
refuses, with a magnificent gesture, to let the men of his household
accompany him to Saragossa – "Best go alone, not slay good men
with me" – are we to take the words at their face-value? Is it not
rather that he does not want witnesses to the treachery that he is
plotting? It is, indeed. Only when, after deliberately working up
the fury of the Saracens to explosion-point, he draws his sword and
"sets his back to the trunk of the pine", do we realise that, so far
from being a coward, he is a cool and hardy gambler, ready to
stake his life in the highly dangerous game he is playing. Even when
at last brought to judgement, he remains defiant, brazenly admitting
the treachery, claiming justification, and spitting out accusa-
tions against Roland. If his nerve fails him, it is not till the last
moment when his own head and hands can no longer serve him,
and he cries to his kinsman Pinabel: "I look to you to get me out
of this!" There is a hint of it, but no more.

Ganelon, like all his sort, is a fluent and plausible liar, but this,
too, we only realise by degrees. His first accusations of Roland
are obviously founded on fact: Roland *is* rash, quarrelsome,
arrogant, and his manner to his stepfather suggests that the dislike is
not all on one side. The tale Ganelon tells Blancandrin (LL. 383–388)

about Roland's boastful behaviour with the apple is entirely in character – invention or fact, it has nothing improbable about it. Ganelon's offensive report of Charlemagne's message (LL. 435–439) certainly goes far beyond the truth, but it may, for all we know, truly express what Ganelon believes to be Charlemagne's intentions; even the further invented details (LL. 474–475) *may* only be "intelligent anticipation". So far we may give Ganelon the benefit of the doubt. But when he returns to the Emperor's camp and explains his failure to bring back the Caliph as hostage (LL. 681–691) by a long, picturesque, and circumstantial story which we know to be a flat lie from first to last, then we know where we are. And after that, we are not inclined to believe in the apple-story, or in Ganelon's alleged wrongs, or in anything else he says.

Similarly, we may accept, and even admire, throughout the council-scene and the scenes with Blancandrin and Marsilion, Ganelon's scrupulous deference and fervent loyalty to the Emperor. If nothing is too bad for Roland, nothing is too good for Charlemagne; this is the voice of the faithful vassal uplifted in praise of his liege-lord. But when the plot has been laid and is going well, then, as he rides homeward with Charlemagne, they hear the sound he never thought to hear again – the blast of Roland's horn. "Listen!" says Charlemagne, "our men are fighting." Ganelon answers with scarcely veiled insolence: "If any man but yourself said this, it would be a lie." And when the Emperor insists, the insolence breaks out undisguised:

> "You're growing old, your hair is sere and white;
> When you speak thus you're talking like a child."

There is in him neither faith nor truth nor courtesy; for all his wit and courage, he is rotten through and through. Yet perhaps he was not always so; he had won the love of his men, and the French held him for a noble baron; there must have been some good in the man before the worm of envy gnawed it all away.

> Before the King stood forth Count Ganelon;
> Comely his body and fresh his colour was;
> A right good lord he'd seem, were he not false.

So the poet sums him up and leaves him.

The portrait of Charlemagne is partly stylised by a number of legendary and numinous attributes belonging to his status as the sacred Emperor. The holiness of the Imperial function, handed down from Constantine through Justinian to the emperors of the West, hovers about him still. He is of unfathomable age – or rather, he is ageless and timeless, for his son and nephew are both young men: his flowing white beard, his strength unimpaired by "two hundred years and more", are hieratic and patriarchal in their symbolism; he is God's vicegerent, the Father of all Christendom, the earthly image of the Ancient of Days.[1] Angels converse with Charlemagne, and the power from on high over-shadows him.

Beneath this larger-than-life-size figure, we discern another: the portrait of the ideal earthly sovereign – just, prudent, magnanimous, and devout. In Charlemagne, the poet has done his best to depict for us the early-mediaeval notion of what we should now call a "constitutional" monarch. He "is not hasty to reply"; he does nothing except by the advice of his Council; he has (it seems) the right to veto any proposition before it has been put to the vote, but once it has received the unanimous assent of the Council, he is bound by that decision, whether he personally approves of it or not. In this, he is carefully contrasted with the Saracen king Marsilion, who conducts most of his negotiations himself, and is at one point restrained with difficulty from throwing his javelin at an ambassador; and also with the Emir Baligant, who, when he calls a Council, merely announces his own intentions, whereupon the councillors advise him to do what he has already said he is going to do. By some writers, Charlemagne's constitutional behaviour has been reckoned as a sign of weakness; but I do not think that is at all what the poet meant. He appears to consider it very proper conduct in a monarch, though we may be doubtful about the extent to which it reflects the behaviour of any actual monarch in the

1. The ceremonial beard and the exterior marks of great age linger on for a long time in literature as the conventional expression of paternal authority. We do wrong to enter into realistic calculations about the respective ages of Cordelia and Lear, Juliet and Old Capulet; the "aged father", like the aged king, is a semantic device, which may be used either to inspire reverence, or, in the customary comic reversal of order, to make a mock of reverence.

feudal era. It comes much nearer to that of an English sovereign today, giving his assent to a bill duly passed by both Houses; he may doubt its wisdom, but he will not for that reason withhold his signature.

Beneath all this again is the personal character of Charlemagne – his stately bearing, his courtesy, his valour and strength, his deep religious feeling, his friendship for Naimon, his warm affection for his nephew and the Peers, and all the "young bachelors" whom he calls "his sons". He rides and fights among his barons as the greatest baron of them all.

Here too, I think we must not reckon it weakness in him that he is overcome by grief for Roland's death, that he faints upon the body and has to be raised up by the barons and supported by them while he utters his lament. There are fashions in sensibility as in everything else. The idea that a strong man should react to great personal and national calamities by a slight compression of the lips and by silently throwing his cigarette into the fireplace is of very recent origin. By the standards of feudal epic, Charlemagne's behaviour is perfectly correct. Fainting, weeping, and lamenting is what the situation calls for. The assembled knights and barons all decorously follow his example. They punctuate his lament with appropriate responses:

> By hundred thousand the French for sorrow sigh;
> There's none of them but utters grievous cries.

At the end of the next laisse:

> He tears his beard that is so white of hue,
> Tears from his head his white hair by the roots;
> And of the French an hundred thousand swoon.

We may take this response as being ritual and poetic; grief, like everything else in the Epic, is displayed on the heroic scale. Though men of the eleventh century did, in fact, display their emotions much more openly than we do, there is no reason to suppose that they made a practice of fainting away in chorus. But the gesture had their approval; that was how they liked to think of people behaving. In every age, art holds up to us the standard pattern of exemplary conduct, and real life does its best to conform. From

Charlemagne's weeping and fainting we can draw no conclusions about his character except that the poet has represented him as a perfect model of the "man of feeling" in the taste of the period.

Compared with the subtleties of Ganelon, Roland's character is simplicity itself. Rash, arrogant, generous, outspoken to a fault, loyal, affectionate, and single-minded, he has all the qualities that endear a captain to his men and a romantic hero to his audience. He has no subtlety at all; other men's minds are a closed book to him. He refuses at first to believe in Ganelon's treachery, and when the truth is forced upon him he can only suppose that the crime was committed "for gold". He never really understands why Oliver is angry with him, nor how much his own pride and folly have contributed to the disaster of Roncevaux. He has the naïve egotism of an Achilles, which will wreck a campaign for a piece of personal pride; but he is a much pleasanter person than Achilles. He never sulks or bears a grudge; he endures Oliver's reproaches with a singular sweetness of temper. Beneath all his "over-weening" there is a real modesty of heart, and a childlike simplicity of love and loyalty – to God, to the Emperor, to his friend, to his men, to his horse, his horn, his good sword Durendal. His death-scene is curiously moving.

But the picture that remains most vividly with us is that of gay and unconquerable youth. No other epic hero strikes this note so ringingly:

> Through Gate of Spain Roland goes riding past,
> On Veillantif, his swiftly-running barb;
> Well it becomes him to go equipped in arms,
> Bravely he goes and tosses up his lance,
> High in the sky he lifts the lancehead far,
> A milk-white pennon is fixed upon the shaft,
> Whose falling fringes whip his hand on the haft.
> Nobly he bears him, with open face he laughs;
> And his companion behind him follows hard.
> The Frenchmen all acclaim him their strong guard.
> On Saracens he throws a haughty glance,
> But meek and mild upon the men of France,
> To whom he speaks out of a courteous heart—

So he rides out, into that new-washed world of clear sun and glittering colour which we call the Middle Age (as though it were middle-aged), but which has perhaps a better right than the blown summer of the Renaissance to be called the Age of Re-birth. It is a world full of blood and grief and death and naked brutality, but also of frank emotions, innocent simplicities, and abounding self-confidence – a world with which we have so utterly lost touch that we have fallen into using the words "feudal" and "mediaeval" as mere epithets for outer darkness. Anyone who sees gleams of brightness in that world is accused of romantic nostalgia for a Golden Age which never existed. But the figure of Roland stands there to give us the lie: he is the Young Age as that age saw itself. Compared with him, the space-adventurers and glamour-boys of our times, no less than the hardened toughs of Renaissance epic, seem to have been born middle-aged.

"Roland is fierce, and Oliver is wise." Oliver is Roland's "companion" – brought up with him, according to the practice of the time, sharing his pursuits and training – and he displays something of that blunt, hard-headed common-sense which is the traditional characteristic of the "hero's friend". Wisdom, in the sense of practical prudence, is a valuable, but not a showy or perhaps a very endearing quality. It is the disastrous Mary Stuarts of history, not the cautious and thrifty Elizabeth Tudors, who flame their way through the pages of ballad and romance. Oliver is a sounder soldier than Roland – more concerned with military necessities than with his own prestige. He mounts a hill before the battle to find out how many enemies they have to reckon with – an action which, by *chanson de geste* standards, scarcely becomes a gentleman; finding the odds unreasonable, he urges Roland to summon assistance – a thing which that hero considers to be beneath his dignity. He goes grimly and gallantly to a task which he knows to be impossible, but he cherishes no illusions, and is unromantic enough to feel no pleasure in the knowledge that "someone had blundered". He has not Roland's sunny disposition; he is capable of cherishing resentment, and when his forebodings have proved all too true, he has a regrettable tendency to say, "I told you so":

> "Companion, you got us in this mess.
> There is wise valour, and there is recklessness;
> Prudence is worth more than foolhardiness.
> Through your o'er-weening you have destroyed the French;
> Ne'er shall we do service to Charles again.
> Had you but given some heed to what I said,
> My lord had come, the battle had gone well,
> And King Marsile had been captured or dead.
> Your prowess, Roland, is a curse on our heads."

Only too true. Is it a little ungenerous to rub it in like this in the moment of disaster? Perhaps; but it is very natural. Responsibility yoked with irresponsibility, however brilliant, has been known to speak its mind thus. A good many married women will sympathize with Oliver.

He has his own pride. It flashes out, sullen and embittered, when Roland, seeing the rear-guard reduced from twenty thousand men to sixty, proposes at long last to summon Charlemagne. "When I told you to do it, you would not; if you had, you would have saved the day and saved our men. To do it now (i.e. when there is nobody to save but ourselves) would be shameful." The Archbishop intervenes, saying that although nobody can now be saved, Charlemagne can avenge them and give them all Christian burial. To this excellent argument Oliver submits in silence. He is a very reasonable young man.

The figure of Archbishop Turpin is "historical" in the same sense that those of Charlemagne and Roland are historical; that is to say, there actually was an Archbishop Tilpinus of Rheims at the end of the eighth century, but his portrait in the poem probably owes more to imagination than to fact. Not that it is an altogether impossible portrait – the warrior-priest is not unknown to Christian history; but Turpin is surely *hors concours*, both for prowess and for personal charm. The poet treats him with very special honour: in the first assault of the Saracens he is given a distinguished place, immediately after Roland and Oliver (LL. 1243 *sqq*); in the second assault he has the honour of "opening the battle" (L. 1487); and he is the last left to stand beside Roland when all the rest are slain. Turpin belongs to an age, which, when the *Song of Roland* was made, was already passing – an age when the secular priest lived very close to the laity. At a later period, Turpin's slighting reference to the life of the cloister (LL. 1880–1882) ,would have come very oddly from an Archbishop's lips; "evidently", as Marc Bloch remarks, "the Gregorian reform had not yet got round" to our poet. Yet, when the French cry: "Well doth our Bishop defend us with his crook!" (or, more literally, "In our Archbishop the crozier is strong to save"), the words are meant in a double sense. With all his fighting qualities, Turpin is a good churchman and a good pastor. He is wise in council; with strong good sense and mild but firm authority he composes the quarrel between Roland and Oliver; his address to the troops is a model of brevity and simple piety, and he takes his priestly duties seriously; his last dying action is a heroic attempt to aid another. There is something peculiarly touching in Roland's lament for him:

> "Ah, debonair, thou good and noble knight!
> Now I commend thee to the great Lord of might;
> Servant more willing than thee He shall not find.
> Since the Apostles no prophet was thy like
> For to maintain the Faith, and win mankind.
> May thy soul meet no hindrance in her flight,
> And may Heav'n's gate to her stand open wide!"

This is perhaps the right place at which to speak of the essential Christianity of the poem. It is not merely Christian in subject; it is Christian to its very bones. Nowhere does the substratum of an older faith break through the Christian surface, as it does, for example, in *Beowulf*. There is no supernatural except the Christian supernatural, and that works (as being fully Christian it must) only to influence men's minds and actions, and not to provide a machinery for the story. And it is a Christianity as naïve and uncomplicated as might be found at any time in the simplest village church. These violent men of action are called on to do their valiant duty to the Faith and to the Emperor; and when they die, they will be taken to lie on beds of flowers among – strangely but somehow appropriately – the Holy Innocents, in a Paradise inhabited by God and His angels. They make their prayers directly to God Himself – no saints are invoked, not even, I think, the Mother of God; it is as simple as that.

Simplicity does not mean ignorance. The poet is not likely to have been a monk or an ecclesiastic in major orders, but he was "clerkly" enough to be acquainted with the lections and liturgy of the Church, and his theology, so far as it goes, is correct. But like most of his Christian contemporaries he has only the vaguest ideas about the Moslem religion. For him, Saracens are just "Paynims" (i.e. Pagans) and therefore (most inappropriately) idolaters. They worship an "infernal trinity", very oddly made up of Mahound (Mohammed), Termagant (a diabolic personage of obscure origin) and – rather unexpectedly – Apollo, who is in process of degenerating into the "foul fiend Apollyon" familiar to us from *The Pilgrim's Progress*. The images of these "false gods" are carried before the Saracen armies, and worshipped on bended knees; when disaster overtakes the Paynim cause they are abused, and maltreated after the manner of savage fetishes. The "law" (i.e. doctrine) of "Mahound and Termagant" is contained in a book, though it is not clear whether the poet is aware of the existence of the Koran, or is merely supposing, on the analogy of the Bible, that every religion must have a sacred book of some kind. (That the ignorance was mutual may be seen by anybody who cares to examine the account of Christian worship and customs given in parts of the *Thousand Nights and a Night*.)

Some slight attempt is made to differentiate Oriental manners from those of the Occident. The Paynim King, Marsilion, holds his council lying down on a dais or divan, whereas Charlemagne sits upright on a faldstool (chair, or throne); the use of darts and other throwing-weapons is confined to the Saracen armies; and the description of the taking of Saragossa suggests that the poet had in mind the great walled cities of Moslem Spain, where the art of fortification was much more advanced than in Northern Europe. It is also perhaps significant that the Emir Baligant is made to promise his warriors not only booty but "fair women" as the reward of valour. Generally speaking, however, Moslem society is deemed to conform more or less closely to that of the West, and is credited with much the same kind of feudal structure. Nor is the

Christian poet ungenerous to the enemy. Marsilion is, of course, treacherous, and the autocracy of the Emir is contrasted with the "constitutional" monarchy of Charlemagne; but prowess and personal courage are plentiful on both sides, and though many of the Saracen champions hail from sinister and mysterious territories abounding in devils and sorcerers, they make no unfair military use of magical aids; it is all good, clean fighting. The great and chivalrous figure of Saladin had not yet risen up to compel the admiration of the Franks, but the reputation of the Moslem fighter stood high, and is ungrudgingly admitted:

> From Balaguet there cometh an Emir,
> His form is noble, his eyes are bold and clear,
> When on his horse he's mounted in career
> He bears him bravely armed in his battle-gear,
> And for his courage he's famous far and near;
> Were he but Christian, right knightly he'd appear.

Roland and his Peers are not merely overwhelmed by numbers; they are given foemen worthy of their steel. This is as it should be; you cannot make an epic out of a conflict where all the heroic qualities are on one side.

The battle-scenes are described with immense relish and, from our point of view, at rather tedious length. We must remember that for mediaeval people warfare was not only a calling but the greatest of all sports. They enjoyed the details of fights and the enumeration of the various warriors engaged as we today enjoy a running commentary upon a Test Match or a Cup-Tie Final, with biographical notes upon the players.

The fighting is all done upon horseback, and only the "noble" weapons of spear and sword are employed. There is no mention of foot-soldiers, or of the archers who played so large a part in the Battle of Hastings. This is partly due to the epic convention, but it is also historically true that at this period the most important part in a battle was played by the cavalry charge. Neither was it in fact very desirable to encumber an army with great numbers of infantry, especially in a foreign country; speed of movement was essential when long distances had to be traversed over few and bad roads, with poor facilities for transport and victualling.

Of the activities of the rank-and-file we are not told much, beyond that, in a general way, "the French" or "the Paynims" exchange good blows in the mellay; the emphasis is all placed on personal encounters between the leaders on either side. We shall notice the same thing in sober historical accounts of mediaeval battles. This, again, is not merely a convention, still less is it (as some writers would have us believe) the manifestation of an "undemocratic" spirit or a contempt for the common man. There was a very practical reason for it. Under the feudal system, it was the duty of every great lord to serve the King in battle, bringing with him so many armed vassals, each of whom in turn brought so many lesser vassals of his own, and so on down the whole scale of hierarchy. Each vassal was bound by oath of allegiance to his own lord and to his own lord only, "while their lives should last"; consequently, if a great lord was killed in battle, his followers were automatically released from their allegiance; they could – and some did – retire from the conflict and take no more part in it. Similarly, if he was taken prisoner or fled from the field, they were left without leader and tended to disintegrate.[1] Hence it was of enormous importance that a lord should lead his men boldly, fight with conspicuous bravery and (if possible) not get killed, or even unhorsed, lest his followers should lose sight of him and become discouraged. This is why Ganelon is so insistent that, if only Roland can be got rid of, the flower of the French army, most of whom are Roland's vassals, will melt away; and this is why, when Marsilion is wounded and flees, the whole Saracen army turns tail. Similarly, when, in the final great battle, the Emperor Charlemagne and the Emir Baligant, lord of all Islam, meet face to face, the whole

---

1. The situation is made very clear in the *Geste* called the *Chanson de Willame*. Here, the cowardly Count Esturmi flees before the battle begins, and his followers, showing an excellent spirit, call on Count Vivian to lead them. Vivian replies that he will gladly do so, but that he sees one great objection:

> "You're not my vassals, and I am not your lord;
> Should you desert me you would not be forsworn."

Esturmi's vassals see the force of this, and at once regularise the position by taking a personal oath to follow him loyally "as long as you shall live".

issue of the war hangs upon their encounter. Baligant falls; and the entire Paynim army at once flees the field.

The poem is called *The Song of Roland*, but only the first half of it deals with the exploits of Roland himself. He dies (L. 2396) at the end of his great stand with the rear-guard against the treacherous assault of King Marsilion.[1] The remainder of the story is concerned with the vengeance which Charlemagne takes for his death, and for the slaughter of the other eleven Peers and the twenty thousand French who are slain with them. By the standards of the time, the tale would be left incomplete without the vengeance, and the name of Charlemagne would be left under a cloud, for to allow the slaying of one's vassal or kinsman to go unavenged was held to be a very shameful thing.[2] But there is more to it than that; there is a question which concerns the whole scope and function of epic, and of the *Roland*'s right to bear that majestic title.

When, as an undergraduate, I first "did" *The Song of Roland*, I accepted easily enough the then-fashionable verdict upon the second part of the poem. "I cannot", said Gustave Lanson,[3] "but range myself on the side of those who think that the revenge of Charlemagne upon the Emir Baligant and his Marsilion is a shabby (*mesquin*) addition, designed to flatter national vanity at the expense of the poetry." Re-reading the poem, after an interval of forty years, for the purpose of translating it, I have found it quite impossible so to range myself.

What has happened in the interval has been, for one thing, the change-over from the "Romantic" notion of the nature and aim of epic poetry to a much more "Classical" conception. At the turn of the century, attention still tended to focus itself narrowly upon the charm of sympathetic personalities and the exploiting of pathetic situations: the reputation of the *Iliad* rested upon the parting of Hector and Andromache, the meeting between Priam

1. Note that he does not die by any Paynim hand – his person is too sacred – but as a result of his own superhuman exertions.

2. Compare the structure of Shakespeare's *Julius Caesar*, which, in the same way, is the story of a murder, duly and correctly followed by a vengeance.

3. *Histoire de la Littérature Française* (1894) p. 25.

and Achilles, and other such selected "beauties"; the *Aeneid* was valued for the sorrows of Dido; the *Divine Comedy* for the Paolo and Francesca episode and the pleasing horror of Ugolino in the Tower of Famine. The wider theme and structure of these monumental works received comparatively little recognition: one ploughed through the bulk of the story for the sake of the "poetical" passages. This point of view still survives in the minds of many film-directors, and of those who produce potted versions of classical novels, or present us with Homer and the Bible in terms of comic-strip technique; and those who most deprecate its latest results would do well to remember that, like many another seedy degenerate, it can boast a highly respectable ancestry. But it is no longer possible for serious criticism to adopt the Romantic attitude; it is committed once more to considering the poem as a whole.

Now if we examine Lanson's statement in the light of the *Roland* itself, we shall notice that he has actually got the facts the wrong way round. It is not the second part of the poem but the first that appeals to national vanity. The famous rear-guard is composed entirely of "Frenchmen of France"; when Marsilion asks on whom Charlemagne relies for his military victories, Ganelon answers: "Upon the French"; the Emperor in council "does nothing but by advice of the French." The war itself is at first presented to us as a struggle for power between (admittedly) Saracen Spain and Christian France, but, for all that, chiefly between Spain and France. It is only when the flower of the French chivalry lies dead in Roncevaux, and Marsilion has fled, mortally wounded, to Saragossa, that there loom up behind the figures of the French champions and the Spanish King the more august images of Emperor and Emir, West and East, Christ and Islam. The world expands before our eyes: we look beyond Saragossa to Alexandria and fabled Babylon; "from forty kingdoms" Baligant summons his powers. And now, embattled alongside the French, for the first time we see "the Franks", and hear the voice of all Christendom. In the final encounter of the last great battle Charles and Baligant meet face to face:

> Quoth the Emir: "Bethink thee, Charles, and see
> That thou repent what thou hast done to me.

My son is slain; I know it was by thee;
And on my lands thou wrongfully hast seized.
Become my man, and I will be thy liege;
Then come and serve me, from here unto the East."
Quoth Carlon: "Nay, I'd hold it treachery;
Never to Paynims may I show love or peace.
Do thou confess the Faith by God revealed,
Take Christendom, and thy first friend I'll be.
The King Almighty then serve thou and believe."
Quoth Baligant: "Thy sermon's but ill preached."
Once more with swords they battle, each to each.

At last the word is spoken that should have been spoken long ago: "Never to Paynims may I show love or peace." It should have been spoken at that first disastrous council; but Charlemagne, though his mind and conscience misgive him, takes counsel of the French, and the French, swayed by Naimon and Ganelon, choose to have peace for peace's sake. True, Marsilion has promised, if the military threat is withdrawn, to embrace Christianity and do homage to the Emperor; but is a man who is capable of murdering ambassadors likely to honour this kind of promissory note at three months, or to set very much value upon the life of his own hostages? Charlemagne, when he first heard of the offer, had indicated that he had doubts as to what was really in Marsilion's mind. But in the council, this point is not debated. Roland alone is peremptory against trusting the Saracen an inch; he wants total surrender, on terms imposed by the conqueror. Unhappily, he gives too much the impression of counselling the right course for the wrong reason, and of wanting war for war's sake. Diplomacy has its way; Christendom is forgotten. That is the sin that brings the tragedy about: wordly prudence plays into the teacherous hands of Ganelon and Marsilion; the price is the loss of the Twelve Peers and twenty thousand French. And in the end the issue has to be faced after all; before ever Marsilion sends envoys to the Emperor's camp, Baligant has set sail from Alexandria.

So the grand outline of the poem defines itself: a private war is set within a national war, and the national war again within the world-war of Cross and Crescent. The small struggle at the centre

shakes the whole web. The evil that is done can never be undone.
God is vindicated, Marsilion and Baligant slain, Saragossa taken,
its inhabitants set to choose between death and baptism, Queen
Bramimonda peaceably converted; but Roland is dead, and the
Peers are dead, and to the war between Belief and Unbelief there
is no ending. Marsilion had asked concerning Charlemagne: "He
is old; when will he weary of going to the wars?" And Ganelon
had replied: "Never, while Roland lives. If Roland were dead we
should have peace." It was a lie. Old as he is, and bereft of his best
help, Charlemagne is Christ's vassal still. "Never to Paynims may
I show love or peace." The Angel summons him, and go he
must.

> Small heart had Carlon to journey and to fight;
> "God!" says the King, "how weary is my life!"
> He weeps, he plucks his flowing beard and white.

Here ends the geste—

It ends, like the *Iliad* and *Aeneid*, in a minor key, and on a fall-
ing cadence. I do not think it has anything to fear from the com-
parison.

Once we have seen the thematic structure of the poem, it is
difficult to look upon the Baligant-passages as an "episode" or on
the vengeance-story as an "addition". And even if we consider
only the "poetry", where are we to make the cut? After the death
of Roland? But we have already heard the blast of Olifant and
the sounding of the Imperial trumpets. After the vengeance upon
Marsilion, losing the lament for Roland, losing the death of Alda,
leaving the tale of Ganelon unfinished, missing so much and so
much? I had forgotten, till I read it again, how good and how
vivid the second half of the *Roland* is. The sailing of the Saracen
fleet, whose "unnumbered lanterns and carbuncles ablaze" make
the night beautiful and light up the whole coast of Spain, is brilliant
as the page of an illuminated missal. Marsilion, disgraced and
dying in his high vaulted chamber, surrendering his glove and fief
to Baligant, puts on a dignity he never had in life. The last encounter
of the last battle, when those two terrible old men fight hand to
hand and all earth and heaven stand breathless to see the issue, is a

moment that seems to happen outside time. They are great, they are supernaturally ancient, their beards are "white as any flower on thorn". Charlemagne receives a buffet that goes near to bring him down: the voice of St Gabriel, rallying him, has that tart stringency which distinguishes the Divine word from pious vapourings:

"And what", said he, "art thou about, great King?"

There is an authentic toughness here which St Theresa of Avila would have recognised. The entry into Saragossa, the funeral journey to Blaye, the return to Aix, the death of Alda, the subtle to-and-fro of the pleadings at the trials, the ordeal by battle, the ghastly execution of Ganelon, and the gay little scene of Brami-monda's baptism follow one another with rapid accuracy and with never a wasted word. It would be easy to mistake this speed for hastiness – easy, but superficial. We have done with the private quarrels, the indecisions, the slow progress of debate and intrigue. The events are now God's hammer-blows, and they fall swiftly. It is a common defect in mediaeval narrators to be unable to vary their pace to suit their matter; but this one knows what he is about. Short as it is and simple in its style, the *Song of Roland* achieves epic stature. It is not a romantic anecdote, but a great poem on a great theme.[1]

Of all the great poems in the world, the *Roland* is perhaps the starkest, not only in theme but in treatment. The style is wholly unadorned: direct statement, direct speech; there are scarcely any general reflections. Only here and there a brief apophthegm sums up a situation or points a moral:

1. Looked on thus, as a whole, it has a much greater theme than that of the *Iliad*. This does not mean that it is a greater poem; it is not, by a long way. In style and technique it is primitive, and has nothing to compare with Homer's music and accomplishment. But in depicting, as both poems do, a struggle between two civilisations, the Christian poet is much more con-scious of a serious purpose, and the mainspring of the action is something more important than the recapture of a wife or a quarrel about booty. In virtue of this greater seriousness and self-awareness, the *Song of Roland*, though "primitive" in form, is entitled to take rank with "secondary" epic, and to be compared (from this point of view only) with Virgil and Milton rather than Homer. (For the distinction between "primary" and "secondary" epic, see C. S. Lewis: A Preface to *Paradise Lost*.)

> When it is known no prisoners will be made
> Men fight back bravely, and stubborn is the fray.
>
> Treason destroys itself and others too.

In the whole 4,000 lines there are scarcely more than half-a-dozen short similes, and these, unlike the Homeric simile, are never elaborated for their own sake, but are expressed in the very minimum of obvious and simple words:

> Leopard or lion was ne'er so fierce as he
>
> White is his beard as any flower of spring
>
> Even as the deer before the deerhound flees,
> So before Roland the Paynims show their heels.

The combats succeed one another with little attempt at variety, put together from the same invariable epithets, the same stereotyped lines and half-lines, the same list of mutilations, the same chorus of comment from the bystanders to conclude the laisse; it is the epic convention at its most conventional. All the champions are fierce and valiant, their helmets gemmed with gold, their steeds swift-running, their weapons stout; on the green grass the blood runs clear and bright. The scenery is indicated in a line or two:

> High are the hills, the valleys dark and deep,
> Grisly the rocks and wondrous grim the steeps.
>
> Bright was the day and clearly the sun shone.

Against this background, the blue and white, the scarlet and the gold, the bright byrnies, the painted shields with their bosses of crystal, shine flat and clear-cut like initials miniated upon vellum. If we are determined to find no pleasure but in sophistication and complexity, we had best leave *Roland* alone; it offers to all our tangled speculations only the most summary of solutions: Paynims are wrong, Christians are in the right; courage and loyalty are all that matters; a noble death is the crown of a noble life.

Times change. The great feudal fabric breaks up; the New Learning comes in from the East, and the "gay science" of love from Provence; the castle gives way to the court, and the teller of tales transfers himself from the clamour of the hall to the quiet of the solar. The rough music of the *chansons de geste* falters and fades; assonance gives place to rhyme; the stanzas prolong and repeat themselves, lose shape and fibre, and are replaced by the rhymed couplets, flowing on unchecked, elegant, refined. Charlemagne gives place to Arthur of Brittany, Roland and Oliver to the Knights of the Round Table – to reappear, centuries later, as the absurd and extravagant heroes of Boiardo and Ariosto. By the middle of the twelfth century, Epic is out, and Romance is in. Most of the *chansons de geste* are forgotten now, except by scholars – Guillaume d'Orange, Raoul de Cambrai, the Quatre Fils Aymar, Girart de Viane, the field of Aliscans – who remembers their names? – But the horn of Roland still sounds through the Pass of Roncevaux –

Dieu! que le son du cor est triste au fond des bois.[1]

2. THE FEUDAL PICTURE

THE word "mediaeval" is often loosely used to cover the whole period from the end of the Dark Ages (about the ninth century) to the beginning of the Renaissance (about the sixteenth century), and it is easy to get the impression that throughout that period European society remained much of a muchness, and was all more or less organized upon the "feudal system". That is not the case, although, of course, relics of feudalism have remained embedded in our social and legal machinery to the present day. But the genuinely feudal organization is already beginning to break up almost everywhere by about the eleventh century (the time when the *Song of Roland* was first written down), to yield to a more centralized type of government under the greatly increased power of the crown. By the middle of the twelfth century the whole face of society has been transformed – there is a new learning, a new literature, a new convention of behaviour as between men and women, new manners, new costumes, new armour, new interests, new developments in church and castle, camp and court.

1. God! how sad is the sound of the horn in the heart of the woods!

A. DE VIGNY

It is of these that we usually think when we hear the phrase "the Middle Ages", because story and picture have made them familiar to us. But the *Song of Roland* belongs to a very much more un-sophisticated period, when the extreme insecurity of life made martial prowess the most necessary of all manly virtues, and it was every baron's business to be a tower of strength to the dwellers on his own land. Thus the feudal structure, as it emerged, rather than was deliberately organized, from the prevailing conditions, was that of a society permanently geared to warfare; and its songs and stories are almost all about brave warriors and heroic deeds in battle – not about ladies or enchanters or other-world adventures, like the romances of chivalry which were to take their place. The world of the French *chanson de geste* is pre-eminently a man's world – more so than the world of Homer, or that of Celtic folk-tale or even of the Scandinavian epic. Occasionally, indeed, a woman makes her appearance – sometimes a strong-minded lady like Guiborc, the wife of Guillaume d'Orange, as capable of keeping her husband's castle in his absence as of cooking him gargantuan meals when he returns from the battlefield; sometimes an unhappy victim of the chances of war, like fair Aude in the *Song of Roland*; sometimes, like the Saracen queen Bramimonda, a spirited woman with but little scope for her energies. But no powerful emotions are focused upon these female characters. The relationships which touch the heart are those which bind the vassal to his lord and the fighting man to his friend and companion in arms. The tie between fellow-soldiers has always been a strong one, and never more so than when war involves absence from home for years at a time, without letters or leave. The relationship between a Roland and an Oliver has the glamour, as well as the depth and devotion, of a love bond. But there is nothing morbid or sentimental about it. The present century has contrived so to cheapen all human relation-ships that it is difficult to find an unambiguous word for this strong blend of affection, admiration, and loyalty between two men. "Friendship" is a little too cool; "mutual hero-worship" a little too adolescent in its over-tones. To us, the most striking thing about it is perhaps the note of grave and formal courtesy which dignifies it from first to last; in grief or joy, in anger or in fondness, in fighting or in dying the mode of address is always: "Fair sir, companion."

In order to clear up a few points which might perplex the reader when surveying the picture of the feudal world presented to us in the poem, I have assembled here one or two explanations which would have unduly burdened the footnotes. Details about clothing and armour have in the same way been gathered together for me by my friend Miss Norah Lambourne, who has illustrated them by drawings, which will, we hope, enable the reader to picture the incidents of the battle, and the characters in their habit as they lived (see pp. 48–49).

3. VASSALAGE

THE social structure of the feudal age was founded upon vassalage. This was, at any rate in its origins, a *personal* bond of mutual service and protection between a lord (*seigneur*) and his dependant, and was affirmed by an oath and the rite of "homage". The vassal placed his hands, joined, as in prayer, between the hands of the lord, and swore to be "his man" (*homme*) so long as they both should live; after which the two parties kissed each other upon the mouth.[1] Both parts of the rite clearly symbolize the reciprocity of the relationship – the submissive and the enfolding hands, and the mutual kiss. The vassal undertook to be faithful to his lord, and to serve him in a variety of ways, including (what is chiefly to our purpose here) the duty of following him to war with as many armed men, chosen from his own dependents, as his wealth and rank made obligatory. The duty of the lord was to protect his vassal in life and avenge him in death, to do justice between him and his fellow-vassals, and to maintain and reward him for his services. *Maintenance* was of two kinds. In the one (*provende*), the vassal was taken into the lord's household, where he was lodged, fed, clothed, and generally "provided for" at the lord's expense. Such vassals constituted the lord's "household" or "meinie"

1. The rite of homage, by the hands and the kiss, is still performed at the Coronation of an English sovereign.

(*maisnée*) and stood in a peculiarly personal relationship to him. The other way was called "*chasement*", literally "housing (*casa*)"; the vassal was given a dwelling, that is to say a piece of land, from the revenues of which he was expected to maintain himself. Remuneration for services, particularly remuneration in the shape of a grant of land, was called a "fief" or "feu" – a word which has given its name to the "feudal" system. In process of time, such fiefs became hereditary, but at the beginning of the feudal period they were held only by a life tenure. The granting of a fief was symbolized by the handing-over, before witnesses, of a token – sometimes a written deed, more often a sod of turf, a straw, or (in the case of an important military appointment) a staff or standard: in a German manuscript of the *Rolandslied*, Charlemagne is shown handing Roland a standard in token of his investiture of the Marches of Spain. In the *Chanson de Roland* the token most commonly used for the grant or surrender of a fief is a glove (LL. 2827–2838).

4. TOKENS

THE handing-over of a visible token as the sign of an appointment or agreement is, of course, of very great antiquity, and seems to have had two main purposes. It could be shown as evidence of the authority entrusted to one: "I come from the King; here is his ring, (staff, banner, glove, or what-not) to prove it." This was particularly useful in a society where few people knew how to read. But it was also employed as a means of impressing the occasion upon the memory of participants and bystanders alike. In the same spirit, the wits of youthful witnesses[1] to a transaction were stimulated by a smart box on the ear – as being something that they were not likely to forget in a hurry – and the glove itself may possibly represent a "token buffet" of this kind. The tokens used in the *Roland* include the glove (for a fief, as above), the glove and wand (for the appointment of an envoy, or messenger), and

---

1. Witnesses were usually chosen as young as possible in order that they might survive the longer to give their testimony in case of subsequent dispute. The place of the buffet was sometimes taken by a small gift of some kind, or, more drastically, by forcible immersion in cold water.

the bow which Charlemagne hands to Roland when appointing him the command of the rear-guard.

5. CHIVALRY

As used in the poem, the words "knight", "chivalry" (*chevalier, chevalerie*) do not necessarily mean men who have been admitted, by dubbing with the sword, into a formal "order" of knighthood. Neither, in spite of the derivation from *cheval*, do they simply correspond to our "horseman, cavalry". A *chevalier* is always a mounted warrior, but not every mounted warrior is a *chevalier*, for squires, sergeants, and the greater part of the army marched, and many of them also fought, on horseback. The distinguishing mark of the *chevalier* is the combination of the war-horse, or destrier, with the full equipment of arms and armour appropriate to a man of wealth and standing: the steel helmet, the metal body-armour (mail hauberk, or byrny reinforced with steel plates), the shield, the spear, and the sword (see Costume-plate 2). A steel mace was sometimes added, though there is no mention of this in the *Roland*. The lower ranks were more lightly equipped, with leathern or quilted body-armour, and their horses were of correspondingly lighter build. Thus a great lord would ride to battle, followed by the knights of his household and the chief vassals belonging to his fief, who would themselves be followed by their own vassals, many of whom might also be of knightly status, and all would be attended by followers of lesser ranks, down to the serfs and peasant-proprietors who owed military service to the lords whose "men" they were. The military service demanded from the tillers of the soil was as a rule confined to a comparatively small number of days in the year, and the defence of home territory. When it came to prolonged campaigns abroad, further inducements had to be offered. The lord was always responsible for his men's food and upkeep when in the field; he might also distribute gifts in cash or kind; but the recompense that everyone, from the highest to the lowest, chiefly looked forward to was the division of the spoils of war. The arms of the vanquished, the ransom of prisoners, the tribute of the conquered, and the wealth of sacked cities, were the rewards of victory – hence the stress laid on booty ("silver and gold, and goodly battle-gear"), upon the valuable gifts (lions and bears, horses and hounds, mules laden with gold) offered by Marsilion as the price of a peace-treaty, and on the richness of all the armour described (helmets gemmed with gold, gold-plated saddles with silver saddle-bows, swords with jewelled hilts, and so forth). We may, however, note that, apart from such references as these, the general tone of the poem, and the behaviour of all the characters, is chivalrous, disinterested, and governed by a strict sense of military propriety: nobody wastes time, as Homeric warriors so often do, by stopping in the middle of a battle to strip the corpse of his adversary. Behind the savage simplicity of the battle-scenes, one feels a strict sense of decorum at work.

6. THE RULES OF BATTLE

"You will observe the Rules of Battle, of course", said the White Knight to the Red Knight; and Alice, you may remember, said to herself as she watched the fight: "One Rule seems to be that, if one Knight hits the other he knocks him off his horse, and if he misses, he tumbles off himself." The Knights would have stood a very poor chance in an eleventh-century battle, where, if you were to survive at all, it was of paramount importance to keep your horse on its legs and yourself on its back. If you were knocked off, or fell off, you ran an imminent risk of either being trampled to death, or having your throat cut by any man-at-arms who happened to be handy. The mediaeval saddle, with its long stirrups, padded seat, and high bows before and behind, was designed to keep you firmly in your place – not, like the modern racing saddle, to enable you to slip easily from a falling horse. The poet expressly mentions (LL. 2031-2034) that when Roland faints in the saddle from pain and loss of blood, "he would have fallen, but was held upright by the stirrups." If the thrust of a spear bore you backwards, you were supported by the saddle-bow behind; if a heavy blow from a sword laid you flat on the horse's neck, you clung to the saddle-bow in front. The bursting of the saddle-girth was a major disaster, bringing you infallibly to the ground. This accident occurs twice in *Roland*, but on each occasion in a single combat and (by a happy symmetry) to both combatants simultaneously, so that they have time and room to extricate themselves and carry on.

We may, however, distinguish certain rules – or it might be better to say, a certain pattern – of battle characteristic of these epic encounters. Something must be allowed for poetic stylisation, but the general outline is probably founded upon actual practice. A fight which goes to its full length, is, ideally, a formal composition in six movements:

1. *The Defiance:* When two combatants meet face to face, the challenger opens the proceedings with a threat or insult (see, e.g. LL. 1238–1242).

2. *The Encounter with the Spear:* In the *Roland*, all the combatants use the spear in the modern fashion (*escrime nouvelle*): the spear is held firmly under the right arm, with the point directed at the adversary's breast or helmet, the aim being either to pierce him through, or to hurl him from the saddle by weight and speed as the horses rush together. In the Bayeux Tapestry, which is roughly of the same date as the *Roland*, both the old (*escrime ancienne*) and the modern fashion are shown together, some knights being depicted with the right arms raised above head-level, using the spear as a throwing-weapon. It will be noticed that the spears thus thrown have plain shafts, whereas most of those used in the modern *escrime* are adorned with a pennon or gonfalon just below the point, exactly as described in the *Roland* (e.g. LL. 1228, 1539, 1576, etc).

3. *The Encounter with the Sword (a) on Horseback:* If the spears are shattered without decisive result, and no squire is at hand to supply fresh ones, the combatants draw their swords to continue the fight. The sword of the period was a single-handed weapon, but it was not unusual to take both hands to it in order to deliver a particularly heavy blow, letting loose the bridle, and leaving the trained destrier to do his own work. The edge, not the point, of the blade was used, the weapon being brought down, if possible, on the opponent's head. If the blow was parried, or glanced off the steel helm, it might light upon the shoulder, inflicting a mortal wound or disabling the right arm. It is by a glancing blow of this

kind that Roland severs Marsilion's right hand at the wrist and puts him out of action. (LL. 1902–1903).

The Encounter with the Sword (b) on Foot: If the combatants are unhorsed and are able to scramble to their feet, the sword-fight is continued on foot by the same method of hacking and hewing.[1]

4. *The Mutual Summons to Surrender:* In a prolonged single combat, such as that between Charlemagne and Baligant (LL. 3564–3624), or in the formal Trial by Ordeal of Battle between Thierry and Pinabel (LL. 3873–3930) there is often a pause to recover breath. This is the moment at which it is proper for each combatant to summon the other to surrender upon terms. If both refuse, the fight is continued till one or other is vanquished.

5. *The Death-Blow:* When one adversary is disarmed or otherwise put out of action, the victor either summons him to surrender at discretion, or delivers the death-blow. In the *Roland*, every fight is to the death (*à outrance*), it having been announced (L. 1886) that no prisoners will be taken.

6. *The Victor's Boast:* Having killed your enemy, you encourage yourself and your men by hurling insults at his dead body. This custom is not altogether in accordance with English notions of sportsmanship, but is part of the correct procedure in all early epic. In Homer, the Boast, like the Defiance, is often elaborated into a lengthy speech; in the *Roland*, it consists as a rule only of a line or so, hardly amounting to more than the "Take that, you b—!" which even modern standards may allow to be excusable in the heat of conflict. (See, e.g. LL. 1232, 1253–1257, 1296).

Needless to say, it was held treacherous and unknightly to attack a man from behind. Oliver, Roland's companion, and too peerless

1. If you unhorsed your opponent without falling yourself, it was sometimes prudent as well as chivalrous to dismount also, lest he should kill or disable your mount. This situation does not occur in the *Roland*, but in the *Geste* of the *Couronnement de Louis*, the hero, Guillaume Court-nez, is particularly praised for his valour in that, when contending on foot against a mounted adversary, he refrains from attacking the horse. To do so would be the obvious way of lessening the odds against him, but he would consider it unknightly behaviour – and besides, he wants the horse himself, having lost his own!

a champion to be allowed by the poet to perish in a straight fight, is killed by a foul blow of this kind (L. 1945).

7. NURTURE AND COMPANIONAGE

OVER and above the general bond of vassalage, there are also the special ties which bind a man to the lord who has "nurtured" him, and to the man who is his "companion". It was the ancient custom to send a boy of good family to be brought up ("nurtured", or "fostered") in the household of one's over-lord, where he received such education as was to be had, learned good manners, and was trained in arms, sports, and horsemanship. Two boys thus bred up side by side from early youth, and competing together in their work and play, would become special friends, or "companions"; and this intimacy and friendly rivalry would be continued in after life. The affection between companions, and that between the lord and the lads nurtured in his house was a very strong one, frequently overshadowing those of blood-relationship. Thus we hear of the "young bachelors" of Charlemagne's household, "whom he calls his 'sons' "; and we see how Roland's thoughts in his death-hour go, not only to "the men of his line", but also to "his Lord, Charlemayn, who'd bred him from a child", and in especial to his "companion", Oliver. It will be noticed also that each of the Twelve Peers has a special "companion", so that the names nearly always go together in pairs: Gerin and Gerier, Ives and Ivor, Othon and Berenger, Anseis and Sanson; (the remaining pair, Gerard of Roussillon and Engelier of Bordeaux presumably pair off together, though their "companionage" is not specially mentioned – perhaps because Gerard is represented as being an old man).

8. HORSES AND SWORDS

IT is scarcely necessary to point out the importance of, and the affection bestowed upon, those cherished and valuable possessions, a good horse and a good sword. On these, a fighting man's life and reputation depended: to lose one or other was a disaster; to think of either in the enemy's hands was shame and sorrow. Distinguished

horses and swords have honoured names attached to them – and
we notice that the Saracen Emir Baligant bestows a name on his
sword, in order that it shall in no way seem inferior to the sword
of Charlemagne. Here, for handy reference, is a list of the famous
horses and swords in the *Chanson de Roland*, with their owners.

CHRISTIANS

Owner	Horse	Sword
Charlemagne	Tencendur (Strife)	Joyeuse (Joyous)
Roland	Veillantif (Wideawake)	Durendal (? Enduring)
Oliver		Hauteclaire (Highbright)
Gerin	Sorel (Sorrel)	
Gerier	Passecerf (Stag-beater)	
Turpin		Almace [Name of Arabic origin and doubtful meaning]
Ganelon	Tachëbrun (Brownspot)	Murgleys (? Death brand)

PAGANS

Marsilion	Gaignun (Watch-dog)	
Baligant		Précieuse (Precious) (he also has a lance called "Maltet" – "Evil")
Climborin		Barbamouche (Barbary Fly)
Valdabrun		Gramimond (Grim)
Grandoyne		Marmorie (Dapple)
Malquiant		Sautperdu (Wild-leap)

9. THE VERSE AND THE TRANSLATION

LIKE all the early *chansons de geste*, the *Roland* is written in ten-
syllabled lines, grouped together in stanzas (known as laisses) of
irregular length. The final syllables of the lines in every laisse are
not rhymed but assonanced together – i.e. they all have the same
vowel-sound, but no regard is paid to the following consonants,
so that, for example, words like "*Charles, barbe, France*" all have

the same assonance. Any full rhymes that occur – as they frequently do – are merely accidental.

All the lines are heavily end-stopped, and each is divided by a caesura, usually falling after the fourth syllable,

> Charlës li reis,   nostre emperedre maignes
> Carlon the king,   our Emperor Charlemayn

but occasionally after the sixth.

The assonance may be either masculine or feminine,[1] and remains so throughout the laisse; the end of the word preceding the caesura may also be either masculine or feminine, and may vary its gender from line to line, the extra syllable not counting in the scansion.

Although the lines are scanned by syllables and not by stresses, there are in practice at least four stress-accents in every line, one of which always falls on the final syllable and one on the syllable immediately before the caesura. Of the others, one falls before the caesura and one or more after – otherwise they have no fixed place.

It is this shift of the interior accent, and this occasional trip or jolt over the feminine caesura, which give to the measure its curious and characteristic rough rhetorical movement, so well suited for reciting or chanting aloud. In the translation, I have tried to reproduce all these characteristics as closely as possible. The general effect is a little rougher than that of the original, because there is, in modern English, no exact equivalent for the French unstressed e, so that the feminine endings, not being uniform, make the difference between the two kinds of laisse rather more conspicuous than it should be. It has also not been altogether easy to keep the assonance "pure" in those laisses which contain long lists of proper names, and here and there some liberties have had to be taken with spelling and pronunciation to compel the endings into some kind of conformity. Thus "Oliver" may appear at the end of a line as "Olivére", "Othon" as "Othóne" when the assonance requires it. The exigencies of assonance, and the extreme rigidity of the end-stopped line, have also occasionally made it necessary

1. A feminine ending is one in which the stressed syllable which carries the assonance is followed by an unaccented e (Charlës, Francë); a masculine ending is one in which it is not so followed (gant, Rollánt).

to use an archaic word where the modern form was hopelessly unwieldy (e.g. "eme" for "uncle", "County" for "Count", "fere" for "companion"). All such archaisms will be found duly elucidated in a footnote. Allowance being made for these irregularities (which may the reader pardon) the translation will, I think, give a fair idea of the rhythm and movement of the Old French. The best way, if it can be managed, is to take a few laisses and declaim them aloud in the bathroom. Here is a short masculine laisse, with the caesura and tonic stresses marked for the benefit of the reciter:

> Marsílion sát   in Sáragóssa tówn,
> He soúght an ófch(ard)   where sháde was to be foúnd,
> On a bríght dá(is)   of márble he liés dówn;
> By twénty thóu(sand)   his vássals stánd aroúnd.
> He cálls befóre (him)   all his dúkes and his coúnts:
> "Lísten, my lórds,   what afflíction is óurs!
> The Emp'ror Chárles   that wéars fair Fránce's crówn
> Inváides our cóun(try)   our fórtunes to confoúnd.
> I háve no hóst   but befóre him gives groúnd,
> I fínd no fórce   his fórces for to flóut;
> Wise men of wít,   give coúnsel to me nów,
> Sáve me from déath   and lóss of my renówn."
> There's né'er a páy(nim)   útters a single soúnd,
> Till Bláncandrín,   Valfónda's lórd, speaks oút.
>   (LL. 10–23)

In two out of the following six lines, the caesura falls at the sixth syllable:

> Nów are the Páy(nims)   in Sársen haúberks díght
> Whereóf the móst   with tríple malfare líned;
> *Góod Saragóssa hélms   they láce on tíght,*
> *Swórds of Viánna stéel   gírd on their thíghs;*
> Speárs of Valénce   they háve, and shiélds full fíne,
> Their gónfalóns   are scárlet, blúe, and white.
>   (LL. 994–999)

The accent and break at the caesura need not be heavy ones, but they must be perceptible. That is to say, it is not possible to have a line of the type:

>   1   2   3   4   5   6 7 8 9   10
>   Count Roland and Count Oliver are there

in which the fourth syllable falls on a conjunction, and the sixth in the middle of a word. This is the feature which differentiates the line from our own familiar "heroic decasyllable" or "iambic pentameter", and gives it the same stiffness and formality that we find in the classical French alexandrine; while the abrupt end-stopping, which makes every line a detached unit, reduces the whole poem to a pattern of archaic simplicity.

The mysterious letters "AOI" which occur at the conclusion of many laisses have given editors much food for thought. It seems probable that they represent some kind of shouted refrain ("Ahoy!"), analogous to the refrain of a ballad.[1] It will be noticed that the *Roland* has certain other affinities with ballad-structure, in particular the repetitive stanzas (known as "similar laisses") which make their appearance from time to time – usually at the most important and moving moments of the narrative, as for example, where Oliver summons Roland to blow his horn (LL. 1048–1081), or where the poet is describing the death of Roland (LL. 2355–2374). The original statement made in one laisse is repeated a second, third or fourth time, with a fresh set of assonances, and usually with added or varied details. It is not always easy to say whether the poet is saying one thing or three things: in the death-scene, he is clearly describing the same action three times; but in the horn-scene, he may quite well mean that Oliver repeats his summons three times over. However this may be, the resemblance to ballad-technique is quite unmistakable, if we compare it with the Ballad of *Sir Patrick Spens*:

> O lang, lang may the ladies sit
> Wi' their fans intil their hand
> Or e'er they see Sir Patrick Spens
> Come sailin' to the strand.
>
> And lang, lang may the ladies sit
> Wi' their gowd kaims i' their hair,
> A-waitin' for their ain true luves,
> For them they'll see nae mair.

1. Sometimes the scribe omits them, probably by an oversight. Sometimes he puts them in the wrong place; I have silently tidied up the latter anomaly.

Or with the mediaeval carol:

> He came all so still
> Where His Mother was
> As dew in April
> That falleth on the grass.
> He came all so still
> Where His Mother lay
> As dew in April
> That falleth on the spray.

It appears on the whole probable that the ballad, the carol, and the *chanson de geste* all derive ultimately from a common origin, in a dance-song (*carole*), with its repetitive verses and refrain such as we find in *London Bridge*, or *Oranges and Lemons*; but it seems fairly clear that the *chanson de geste* does not derive directly from carol and ballad, nor they from it. Nor can we say (as was once the fashion) that the nobly-constructed *Roland* assembled itself accidentally out of a patch-work of popular song and legend; although no doubt the poet drew his material from "folk legend" and "oral tradition" – whatever those phrases may precisely mean.

And who was the poet? Of all the tantalising riddles in literature, the last line of the *Song of Roland* may bear away the bell. For it dangles a name before us, only to twitch it away just as it seems within our grasp.

> *Ci faut la geste ke Turoldus declinet*
> Here ends the geste which Turoldus – ?

Unhappily, nobody knows exactly what *declinet* means. "Which Turoldus composed"? or "recited"? or merely, in the capacity of a scribe, "copied out"? Does the "geste" mean the poem itself? or does it refer to the alleged chronicle from which the poet claims to have obtained his facts? Does "faut" mean that the poem here comes to its appointed conclusion? Or that the remainder of the poem – or the chronicle – is unfortunately lacking: *caetera desunt*? As for Turoldus, though the name occurs here and there in documents of about the right period, there is nothing to connect any of the persons who bear it with the *Roland* or its fortunes. Even the word "ke" is ambiguous – it probably means "which", but it might mean "since"; and at least one editor has desperately rendered the line: "Here the poem has to end because Turoldus' powers are declining." Faced with this masterpiece of obscurity, the translator must either be misleadingly definite or seek to match ambiguity with ambiguity. I have been as non-committal as I could, but confess that I have failed to produce anything quite so baffling as the original.

I have made no attempt to identify all the outlandish names of places and peoples with which the poet has adorned his tale. Some are probably pure fantasy; others, garbled versions of actual proper names which cannot now be referred with any certainty to their origin. Only here and there, when the name offered some point of interest, have I thought it worth while to append a brief note. It is, however, of some importance to note the distinction between the use of the words "French" and "Franks". The "French" are the men of France proper – the flower of Charlemagne's army, who compose his council, form the famous rear-guard of Roland, and are given the most distinguished places in the great battle against Baligant. (The poet is after all, himself a "Frenchman of France", and this is a French poem). The "Franks", who only take part in the action after the death of Roland, are *all* the subjects of the Christian Emperor, and include the men of Almayn (Germany), Saxony, Bavaria, Friesland, and other provinces, together with those parts of modern France which were then separate duchies, as for example Brittany, Normandy, and Poitou.

Finally, a word about the names of some of the principal characters. When the *Roland* was written, French was still an inflected language. This means that many proper names appear in two forms: a nominative and an accusative. Just as in Latin "Jupiter" and "Jove" are the same person (and for almost exactly the same reason), so in Old French "Charles" and "Carlon" are the same, "Guènes" and "Ganelon", "Marsile" and "Marsilion", "Ives" and "Ivon", etc. These variations are obviously a great help to the translator when dealing with the cramped conditions imposed by the assonance, the caesura, and the strictly end-stopped line, and I have therefore used them freely, without troubling too much about their grammatical function – which indeed, by the eleventh century was already beginning to be lost. Once warned, the reader will not, I hope, find that they present any very great difficulty. Where no advantage was gained by variation I have generally used the accusative form, or else (as in "Roland") the familiar English equivalent.

The text here translated is that known as the "Oxford Manuscript" (Bodleian Library, Digby 23), which is the oldest and best of all the versions of *Roland*. I have used Bédier's edition of 1922, with considerable help from that of F. Whitehead (1942). In the numbering of the laisses I have followed Bédier, except that I have restored laisses 125 and 126 to the order in which they appear in the MS. Square brackets indicate where missing or defective passages have been conjecturally emended or supplied from other versions of the poem. I have also followed Bédier's example in reducing here and there to a uniform historic present the poet's indiscriminate mixture of present, perfect, and preterite within the same passage and even within the same sentence. Sometimes these changes of tense add vigour; at other times they seem to be due to mere caprice, or to the exigences of the assonance; I have therefore ventured to remove them wherever they tend, in English ears, to cause awkwardness or to hold up the pace of the verse.

DOROTHY L. SAYERS

ACKNOWLEDGEMENTS

MY first debt of gratitude is, of course, to my old tutor, the late Mildred K. Pope, with whom I read the *Roland* at Oxford, and to whom I owe such Old French scholarship as I possess. Unhappily, she did not live to see this translation published, but she gave it every encouragement and much practical help. My thanks are also due to Brother George Every, S.S.M., to Mr R. W. Southern, and to Mr R. Allen Brown, for valuable advice on special points; and to Dr Joan Evans, Dr Barbara Reynolds, and Dr Lewis Thorpe for their energetic wrestlings with the riddle of Ganelon's "hoese". Most especially, too, I have to thank Dr Thorpe, who patiently vetted the whole translation line by line and saved me from numerous slips and mistakes. Such inaccuracies as may remain are due to my own errors of judgement, when the verse-maker insisted on setting the claims of metre and assonance above those of strict scholarship, and for these my kind and able advisors are in no way to blame.

A NOTE ON COSTUME

GANELON BEFORE THE COUNCIL

CIVIL COSTUME

Note the simple form of dress which consisted of tunic, super-tunic or bliaut, and mantle.

The tunics were often girdled and pulled up and were made of linen or fine wool. The super-tunic was sometimes made of silk when worn by the nobility. Decoration was in the form of woven or embroidered bands round the neck, hem, or sleeves. The sleeves tended to be very long and were often pushed up, thus producing a wrinkled effect on the lower arm.

The mantle was rectangular in shape and was either three-quarter or full length. It was draped about the figure and held in place by a brooch or pair of clasps (or owches) on the shoulder. People of importance often had their mantles lined with fur (note Ganelon's costume in the illustration).

The legs were covered by stockings or by leggings made of strips of material and flat leather shoes were worn on the feet. Heads were normally uncovered and hair styles were short.

THE FRENCH AT RONCEVAUX

MILITARY COSTUME

The armour consisted of a Hauberk, i.e. a long knee-length gar-
ment of chain mail which protected the body and the thighs. The
Byrny was an older form of the Hauberk; it was made of
leather, upon which metal rings were sewn in various patterns.
The helmet with its protective nasal is worn over a chain hood.

Note the strappings from knee to ankle and the short boot and
spurs.

Note also the long pointed shields often with a simple device,
the shape of the saddle, the length of stirrup and the method of
holding the lance as a thrusting weapon (see description in the
text).

THE SONG OF ROLAND

1

CARLON the King, our Emperor Charlemayn,
Full seven years long has been abroad in Spain,
He's won the highlands as far as to the main;
No castle more can stand before his face,
City nor wall is left for him to break,
Save Saragossa in its high mountain place;
Marsilion holds it, the king who hates God's name,
Mahound he serves, and to Apollyon prays:
He'll not escape the ruin that awaits.

AOI

2

Marsilion sat in Saragossa town,
He sought an orchard where shade was to be found,
On a bright dais of marble he lies down;
By twenty thousand his vassals stand around.
He calls before him all his dukes and his counts:
"Listen, my lords, what affliction is ours!
The Emperor Charles that wears fair France's crown
Invades our country our fortunes to confound.
I have no host but before him gives ground,
I find no force his forces for to flout;
Wise men of wit, give counsel to me now,
Save me from death and loss of my renown."
There's ne'er a paynim utters a single sound,
Till Blancandrin, Valfonda's lord, speaks out.

l. 8 *Apollyon* (Apollo) – see Introduction, p. 20, and cf. l. 1392.

3

Blancandrin's wise amid the paynim horde;
He was for valour a mighty knight withal,
And fit of wit for to counsel his lord.
He tells the king; "Be you afeared for naught,
But send to Charles in his pride and his wrath
Your faithful service and your friendship henceforth.
Promise him lions and bears and hounds galore,
Sev'n hundred camels and a thousand mewed hawks,
Four hundred pack-mules with gold and silver store,
And fifty wagons, a wagon-train to form,
Whence he may give his soldiers rich rewards.
Say, in this land he has made enough war;
To Aix in France let him go home once more;
At Michaelmas you'll follow to his court,
There you'll submit unto the Christian law,
And be his man by faith and fealty sworn.
Hostages too, if for sureties he call,
You'll let him have, ten maybe or a score;
'Twere good we send the sons our wives have borne:
I'll send mine own, though he should die therefor.
Better by far the heads of them should fall
Than we should lose honour, estate and all.
And be reduced to beggary and scorn."

                                                    AOI

L. 31 *mewed hawks* – hawks which have got over their moult, and are
consequently in good condition.
L. 34 *soldiers* – these are the mercenaries, who received their pay (*solde*)
directly from the King in cash, as distinct from the feudal vassalage, who
were maintained by their respective lords (see Introduction, p. 31sq). Many
of them were knights-errant, without territorial attachment, who wandered
about offering their services to whoever would employ them.
L. 36 *Aix* – Aix-la-Chapelle was the imperial city of Charlemagne, who
rebuilt its palace and chapel and granted it many special privileges. He was
reputed to have been born there and certainly died and was buried there
in 814.

4

Quoth Blancandrin: "I swear by my right hand
And beard that flutters about my girdle-span,
Straightway you'll see the Frenchman's host disband:
They'll hurry home to France, their native land,
When each within his favourite haunt is back,
Charles in his chapel at Aix will take his stand,
And there he'll hold high feast at Michaelmas.
The time will pass, the trysted hour elapse:
No news of us, no message will he have.
Fierce is the king, a cruel-hearted man;
Our sureties' heads he'll smite off with the axe.
Better their heads should fall into their laps
Than that fair Spain should fall from out our hands,
And we should suffer grave losses and mishap."
The Paynims say: "There is some truth in that."

5

The King Marsile had ended the debate;
He calls before him Clarin of Balagate,
Estramarin, and Eudropin his mate;
And Garlon Longbeard and Priamon he names,
And Machiner and his uncle Matthay,
Johun of Outremer, and Malabayn,
And Blancandrin; these ten make up the tale,
Ten matchless villains, to whom he's said his say:
"Barons, my lords, get you to Charlemayn,
Who sits at siege, Cordova town to take.
Bear each in hand an olive-branch displayed;
Peace and submission are signified that way.
If you contrive this treaty to arrange,
Of gold and silver I'll give you goodly weight,

And lands and fiefs as much as heart can crave."
The Paynims answer: "That will be ample pay."

AOI

6

Marsile the king his conference had ceased.
He tells his men: "My barons, go with speed;
Bear in your hands boughs of the olive tree.
On my behalf King Charlemayn beseech,
For his God's sake to show me clemency.
Say, this month's end in truth he shall not see
Ere I shall seek him with thousand vassals leal.
The law of Christ I'll then and there receive,
In faith and love I will his liegeman be.
I'll send him sureties if thus he shall decree."
Quoth Blancandrin: "Be sure he'll grant your plea."

AOI

7

Marsilion sent for ten mules white as snow,
(A gift that erst Suatilia's king bestowed),
Their saddles silver, their bridles all of gold.
Now are they mounted, the men who are to go;
All in their hands the olive-branches hold.
They came to Carlon that hath France in control;
They'll trap him somehow, for it is fated so.

AOI

8

The Emperor Charles is glad and full of cheer.
Cordova's taken, the outer walls are pierced,
His catapults have cast the towers down sheer;
Rich booty's gone to all his chevaliers,
Silver and gold and goodly battle-gear.

In all the city no paynim now appears
Who is not slain or turned to Christian fear.
The Emperor sits in a great orchard near,
Having about him Roland and Olivere,
Samson the duke, and Anseis the fierce,
Geoffrey d'Anjou the King's gonfalonier,
And Gerin too, and with him too Gerier;
And where these were was many another fere –
Full fifteen thousand of France the fair and dear.
Upon white carpets they sit, those noble peers,
For draughts and chess the chequer-boards are reared;
To entertain the elder lords revered;
Young bachelors disport with sword and spear.
Beneath a pine beside an eglantier
A faldstool stands all of the red gold clear;
Of fairest France there sits the king austere.
White are his locks, and silver is his beard,
His body noble, his countenance severe:
If any seek him, no need to say, "Lo, here!"
From off their steeds lit down the messengers,
Well did they greet him with shows of love sincere.

9

Before them all Blancandrin forward stood;
And hailed the King: "God give His grace to you,
The glorious God to whom worship is due.
Thus speaks the king, Marsilion, great in rule:
Much hath he studied the saving faith and true.
Now of his wealth he would send you in sooth
Lions and bears, leashed greyhounds not a few,
Sev'n hundred camels, a thousand falcons mewed,

L. 108 *fere* – companion.
L. 114 *eglantier* – wild-rose bush.

And gold and silver borne on four hundred mules;
A wagon-train of fifty carts to boot,
And store enough of golden bezants good
Wherewith to pay your soldiers as you should.
Too long you've stayed in this land to our rue:
To Aix in France return you at our suit.
Thither my liege will surely follow you,
[And will become your man in faith and truth,
And at your hand hold all his realm in feu!"]
With lifted hands to God the Emperor sues;
Then bows his head and so begins to brood.

                                        AOI

10

The Emperor bode long time with downcast eyes;
He was a man not hasty in reply,
But wont to speak only when well advised.
When he looked up, his glance was stern and high.
He told the envoys: "Fair is your speech and fine;
Yet King Marsile is foe to me and mine.
In all these words and offers you recite
I find no warrant wherein I may confide."
"Sureties for this", the Saracen replies,
"Ten or fifteen or twenty we'll provide.
One of my sons I'll send, on pain to die;
Others, yet nobler, you'll have, as I divine.
When in your palace high feast you solemnize
To great St Michael of Peril-by-the-Tide,
He'll follow you, on that you may rely,

L. 152 *St Michael of Peril-by-the-Tide* – ("St M. in periculo maris"). The name was originally given to the monastery built on the great island rock called Mont St Michel, off the coast of Normandy. Later it came to be applied to the Archangel himself, "*St Michel del Peril*".

And in those baths God made you by His might
He would turn Christian and there would be baptized."
Quoth Charles: "He yet may save his soul alive."

                                             AOI

11

Fair was the ev'ning and clearly the sun shone;
The ten white mules Charles sends to stall anon;
In the great orchard he bids men spread aloft
For the ten envoys a tent where they may lodge,
With sergeants twelve to wait on all their wants.
They pass the night there till the bright day draws on.
Early from bed the Emperor now is got;
At mass and matins he makes his orison.
Beneath a pine straightway the King is gone,
And calls his barons to council thereupon;
By French advice whate'er he does is done.

                                             AOI

12

The Emperor goes beneath a tall pine-tree,
And to his council he calls his barony:
There Duke Ogier, Archbishop Turpin meet,

L. 154 *baths* – the curative mineral springs for which Aix is still celebrated,
and which were held to be of miraculous origin.
L. 161 *sergeants* – the word "sergeant", meaning primarily "servant", was
applied generally to almost any man, under the rank of knight, who exercised
any kind of office in a lord's household or on his estate. In military use, it
denoted a tenant doing military service, especially one who was in attendance
on a knight in the field. The "sergeant" marched and fought on horseback,
but was more lightly armed than the "chevalier".
L. 170 *Ogier the Dane* – this semi-historical hero boasts a *Chanson de Geste*
devoted to his exploits, and figures in many others.

Richard the Old and his nephew Henri,
Count Acelin the brave of Gascony,
Miles, and his cousin the Lord Tibbald of Rheims,
Gerin likewise and Gerier are convened;
And County Roland, there with the rest came he,
And Oliver, noble and good at need;
All French of France, thousand and more, maybe;
And Ganelon that wrought the treachery.
So starts that council which came to such sore grief.

                                              AOI

13

"Barons, my lords", began the Emperor Carlon,
"From King Marsile come envoys, seeking parley.
He makes me offers of treasure overpassing:
Of lions and bears and hounds to the leash mastered,
Sev'n hundred camels, and falcons mewed and hearty,
Four hundred mules with Arab gold all chargèd,
And fifty wagons well-laden in a cart-train.
But now to France he urges my departure,
And to my palace at Aix he'll follow after,
There change his faith for one of more advantage,
Become a Christian and of me hold his marches.
But his true purpose – for that I cannot answer."
The French all say: "We'd best be very guarded."

                                              AOI

14

The Emperor Charles had finished all his speech.
The County Roland, who fiercely disagrees,
Swift to oppose springs up upon his feet:

L. 171 *Richard the Old* – his historical prototype is Richard I of Normandy, who lived (943–996) later than Charlemagne's time, but has been attracted into the Carolingian cycle by the natural tendency of epic to accumulate famous names regardless of chronology.

He tells the King: "Nevermore trust Marsile!
Seven years long in land of Spain we've been.
I won for you both Noples and Commibles,
I took Valterna, the land of Pine I seized,
And Balagate, and Seville and Tudele.
Then wrought Marsile a very treacherous deed:
He sent his Paynims by number of fifteen,
All of them bearing boughs of the olive tree,
And with like words he sued to you for peace.
Then did you ask the French lords for their rede;
Foolish advice they gave to you indeed.
You sent the Paynim two counts of your meinie:
Basan was one, the other was Basile.
He smote their heads off in hills beneath Haltile.
This war you've started wage on, and make no cease;
To Saragossa lead your host in the field,
Spend all your life, if need be, in the siege,
Revenge the men this villain made to bleed!"

                                        AOI

15

The Emperor Charles sat still with his head bended;
He stroked his beard and his moustaches gently;
Nor good nor ill he answers to his nephew.
The French are silent, Guènes alone excepted;
But he leaps up, strides into Carlon's presence,
And full of pride begins thus to address him.
He tells the King: "Trust not a brawling fellow,
Me nor another; seek only your own welfare.
If King Marsile informs you by this message
He'll set his hands in yours, and fealty pledge you,
And hold all Spain from you, at your good pleasure,
And to that faith we follow give acceptance,

L. 205 *rede* – counsel.

The man who tells you this plea should be rejected
Cares nothing, Sire, to what death he condemns us.
Counsel of pride must not grow swollen-headed;
Let's hear wise men, turn deaf ears to the reckless."

AOI

16

Naimon at this stood forth before them all:
No better vassal was ever seen in hall.
He tells the King: "Well have you heard, my lord,
The arguments Count Ganelon sets forth.
There's weight in them, and you should give them thought.
The King Marsile is vanquished in the war,
You've taken from him his castles and his forts,
With catapults you've broken down his walls,
You've burned his cities and his armies outfought.
Now that he comes on your mercy to call
Foul sin it were to vex him any more.
Since he'll find sureties his good faith to support,
We should make haste to cut this great war short."
The French all say: "The Duke speaks as he ought."

AOI

17

"Barons, my lords, whom shall we send anon
To Saragossa, to King Marsilion?"
"I, by your leave," saith Naimon, "will begone,
Therefore on me bestow the glove and wand."
"You are my wisest", the King makes answer prompt:
"Now by the beard my cheek and chin upon,
You shall not go so far this twelvemonth long.
Hence! sit you down, for we summon you not!"

l. 247 *the glove and wand* – (see Introduction, p. 32).

18

"Barons, my lords, whom shall we send of you
To Saragossa, the Sarsen king unto?"
"Myself", quoth Roland, "may well this errand do."
"That shall you not", Count Oliver let loose;
"You're high of heart and stubborn of your mood,
You'd land yourself, I warrant, in some feud.
By the King's leave this errand I will do."
The King replies: "Be silent there, you two!
Nor you nor he shall on that road set foot.
By this my beard that's silver to the view,
He that names any of the Twelve Peers shall rue!"
The French say nothing: they stand abashed and mute.

19

Then from their ranks arose Turpin of Rheims;
He tells the King: "Leave your French lords at ease;
Full sev'n long years in this land have you been,
Much have they suffered of perils and fatigue;
Pray you then, Sire, give wand and glove to me;
The Saracen of Spain I'll seek and see,
And in his looks his purpose will I read."
The Emperor answers with anger in his mien:
"On that white carpet sit down and hold your peace;
Be still, I say, until I bid you speak."

                                                    AOI

20

The Emperor said: "My free and knightly band,
Come choose me out some baron of my land
To bring my message to King Marsilion's hand."

L. 253 *Sarsen* – Saracen.

Quoth Roland: "Guènes my step-sire is the man."
The French all say: "Indeed, he is most apt;
If he's passed over you will not find his match."
Count Ganelon is furious out of hand;
His great furred gown of marten he flings back
And stands before them in his silk bliaut clad.
Bright are his eyes, haughty his countenance,
Handsome his body, and broad his bosom's span;
The peers all gaze, his bearing is so grand.
He says to Roland: "Fool! what has made thee mad?
I am thy step-sire, and all these know I am,
And me thou namest to seek Marsilion's camp!
If God but grant I ever thence come back
I'll wreak on thee such ruin and such wrack
That thy life long my vengeance shall not slack."
Roland replies: "This is all boast and brag!
Threats cannot fright me, and all the world knows that
To bear this message we must have a good man;
I'll take your place if the King says I can."

AOI

21

Quoth Ganelon: "My place thou shalt not take;
Thou'rt not my vassal, nor I thy suzerain.
Charles for his service commands me to obey.
I'll seek Marsile in Saragossa's gates;
But rather there some deadly trick I'll play
Than not find vent for my unbounded rage."
When Roland heard him, then he laughed in his face.

AOI

22

When Ganelon sees Roland laugh outright
He's fit to burst for anger and despite,
And very nearly goes clean out of his mind.
He tells the Count: "I love you not, not I;
You've picked on me unfairly, out of spite.
Just Emperor, here I stand before your eyes,
Ready to do whatever you think right.

23

To Saragossa I see that I must shift me;
There's no return for him that journeys thither.
Bethink you well that my wife is your sister,
A son she bare me, fairest of goodly children,
"Baldwin" (quoth he) "and a champion he will be.
To him I leave all my lands and my living;
No more I'll see him; take care, Sir, of your kinsman."
Quoth Charles: "Your heart is too tender within you;
Go now you must, for even so I bid you."

AOI

24

Then said the King: "Stand forward, Ganelon,
Here at my hand receive the glove and wand;
You've heard the French – you are the man they want."
"Messire," said Guènes, "Roland hath done this wrong!
I'll never love him the whole of my life long,
Nor Oliver his friend and fellow fond,
Nor the Twelve Peers by whom he's doted on;
Sire, in your presence I defy the whole lot."
Then said the King: "Your passion is too hot;
I bid you go and so you must begone."

"Well may I go, but safeguard have I not,
Basile had none, nor Basan none, God wot."

AOI

25

The King holds out to him his right-hand glove;
Fain would Count Guènes be an hundred miles off!
When he would take it, it fell into the dust.
"God! what is this?" cry all the French at once;
"For sure this message will bring us great ill-luck."
"My lords," quoth Guènes, "you'll know it soon enough."

26

"Sire, give me leave" quoth Guènes, "hence to hie;
Since go I must, it boots not to abide."
"Go", said the King, "by Jesu's leave and mine."
With his right hand he's absolved him and signed,
And to his care letter and wand consigned.

27

Guènes the Count to his lodging makes speed,
Of his array he setteth him to seek
The best he has to serve him for this need.

L. 340 *absolved him and signed* – i.e. pronounced the absolution over him,
making the sign of the cross. Some commentators have seen here a relic
of the very ancient popular conception of the priest-emperor, preserved
in the legend of Prester John. But there is, I think, nothing in the line
which necessarily ascribes *sacerdotal* status to Charlemagne, however
sacred his person and function. What is probably intended is the *prayer* of
absolution, frequently called simply "the Absolution" (as in the Book of
Common Prayer) which can be pronounced by, for example, an abbess, or
indeed any other lay person. It would be some such formula as "The Lord
bless you and keep you, deliver you from all your sins, and bring you to
everlasting life."

His golden spurs he buckles on his heels,
Girds to his side Murgleys his brand of steel,
And mounts him up on Tachebrun his steed;
His stirrup's held by Guinemer his eme.
Then might you see full many a brave knight weep,
Saying to him: "Woe worth your valour's meed!
In the King's court these many years you've been,
A noble vassal by all were you esteemed.
He that named you for this gear by his rede
Charlemayn's self shall not save him nor shield:
No right had Roland to have contrived this scheme;
For you're a man sprung of a noble breed."
Then they said, "Sir, take us with you, we plead."
Guènes replied: "God forbid it should be!
Best die alone nor slay good knights with me.
Sirs, you'll return to fair France presently:
On my behalf my wife I bid you greet,
And Pinabel that is my friend and peer.
Baldwin my son, whom you know well, I ween,
Him shall you help and accept for your liege."
Then he sets forth and on his way goes he.

                                        AOI

28

Under tall olives the County Guènes rides;
The Paynim envoys he's caught up in good time,
And Blancandrin drops back with him behind.
Now each to other begins to speak with guile.
Blancandrin says: "Charles is a wondrous wight!
Pulia he's ta'en, Calabria likewise,
And unto England passed over the salt tide

L. 348 *eme* – uncle.

To win St Peter the tribute of the isle.
What seeks he here, warring in our confines?"
"Such is his pleasure", Count Ganelon replies;
"In all the world you will not find his like."

AOI

29

Quoth Blancandrin: "The French are men of worth,
Yet to their lord they do a scurvy turn,
These dukes and counts, when they counsel such work;
Both him and others they harry to their hurt."
"There's none," quoth Guènes, "who merits such ill words,
Save only Roland, for whom 'twill be the worse.
But now, the Emperor in the cool shade conversed;
Up came his nephew all in his byrny girt,
Fresh with his booty from Carcassone returned.
Roland in hand a golden apple nursed
And showed his uncle, saying, 'Take it, fair sir;
The crowns I give you of all the kings on earth.'
One day his pride will undo him for sure,
Danger of death day by day he incurs.
If one should slay him some peace might be preserved."

AOI

30

Quoth Blancandrin: "Roland's a villain fell,
Presuming thus all folk on earth to quell,
And every land under his yoke compel!
Whom does he count on to lend his arms such strength?"
Ganelon answers: "He counts upon the French;

l. 373 *the tribute of the isle* – The annual tribute known as "Peter's Pence",
paid by England to the See of Rome, was of Anglo-Saxon origin, and
instituted in the eighth or ninth century, though not in consequence of
political or military pressure by Charlemagne.

They'll never fail him, they love him far too well.
Silver and gold he gives them for largesse,
Horses and mules, silks and accoutrements.
And everything the Emperor wants, he gets —
He'll win for him all lands 'twixt east and west."

AOI

31

So long rides Guènes with Blancandrin that day
Till each to each has pledged his truth and faith
They will seek means Count Roland for to slay.
So long they ride, they come by road and way
To Saragossa, and by a yew draw rein.
A faldstool stood beneath a pine-tree's shade,
With silken cloth of Alexandria draped;
There sat the King that bore the rule in Spain.
Full twenty thousand Saracens stood arrayed.
Not one of them has any word to say,
So eagerly upon the news they wait.
And here come Guènes and Blancandrin apace!

32

Blancandrin came before Marsilion,
And by the hand held County Ganelon;
Saith to the King: "Save you, sir, by Mahond,
And by Apollyon, whose blest faith we extol!
To Charles we gave your message every jot;
Both of his hands he lifted up aloft
And praised his God; further, he answered not.
One of his nobles, you see, he's sent along —
A lord of France, of most illustrious stock;
From him you'll hear if peace is won or lost."
"We'll hear him," quoth Marsile; "let him say on."

AOI

33

Now Ganelon had giv'n this matter thought,
And with great cunning he now begins to talk,
Even as a man that's to the manner born.
He tells the King: "God have you in His ward,
The glorious God whom we ought to adore!
King Charlemayn, the Great, thus sends you word:
You must receive the faith of Christ Our Lord,
And as your fief half Spain he will award.
If you refuse to accept this accord,
You shall be taken and fettered by main force,
And haled away to Aix, into his court,
There to be doomed and done with once for all;
There shall you die in shamefulness and scorn."
On hearing this Marsile was quite distraught;
He held a dart with golden feathers wrought,
And would have struck him, but he was overborne.

AOI

34

The King Marsile has all his colour changed.
Grasping the shaft, his javelin he shakes.
When Guènes sees it he sets hand to his blade,
Two fingers' breadth forth of the scabbard hales,
And says to it: "Full bright you are and brave!
In the King's court I've borne you many a day!
Ne'er shall the Emperor of France have cause to say
I died alone in strange lands far away;
Before their bravest the price of you have paid!"
The Paynims cry: "We must prevent this fray."

35

The wiser Paynims remonstrate with him so
That King Marsile has sunk back on this throne.
Quoth the Caliph: "You put us to reproach,
Thinking to threaten this Frenchman with a blow!
It is your business to listen and take note."
Saith Ganelon: "All this, sir, must I thole.
For all the gold God made, I'll not forgo,
No, not for all the wealth your land can boast,
To speak the message – so I'm but given scope –
Which Charles the King, that mighty man of mould,
Has sent by me to this his mortal foe."
He had on him a sable-fur-lined cloak
Covered with silk which Alexandria wove;
He flings it down for Blancandrin to hold,
But of his sword he nowise will let go;
In his right hand he grasps the hilts of gold,
The Paynims say: "Lo there a baron bold!"

                                                    AOI

36

Guènes approached the King and thus addressed him:
He saith to him: "You do vainly to vex you.
Carlon thus bids you, that hath France in possession:
The Christian faith must of you be accepted,
And one half Spain he will give you in tenure;
The other half is for Roland his nephew;
A right proud partner you'll have there for co-tenant!
If these conditions should by you be rejected,
In Saragossa he'll besiege and invest you,
And by main force you shall be seized and fettered.
Thence to his city of Aix you'll go directly.

ℓ. 456 *thole* – endure.

You shall not ride on palfrey nor on destrier,
Nor for the road shall you have mule nor jennet;
On some poor screw of a pack-ass he'll set you;
And you will lose your head there by his sentence.
See now, the Emperor has written you this letter."
To the right hand of the Moor he presents it.

37

The King Marsile for very rage went white;
He breaks the seal and flings the wax aside,
Looks at the letter and reads what is inside.
"These words to me Carlon the French King writes:
I'm to remember his grief and his despite
For those two brothers, Basan and Basil hight,
Whom I beheaded in Haltoye-on-the-Height;
And if I value the purchase of my life,
Must send my uncle the Caliph as his prize;
Else nevermore will he be friend of mine."
Marsilion's son at this broke in and cried:
"Ganelon's words are madness out of mind!
This is too much – he shall not rest alive;
Give him to me and justice he shall find!"
When Guènes heard, he shook his blade on high,
And set his back to the trunk of the pine.

38

Unto the orchard the King Marsile repairs;
Of his best men he takes with him a share,
And thither came Blancandrin white of hair,
And Jurfaret, who is his son and heir,
And the Caliph, his eme and officer.
Quoth Blancandrin: "Call in that Frenchman there:

He'll serve our ends, to this I've heard him swear."
"Fetch him yourself, 'twere best", the King declares.
In his right hand Count Ganelon he bare
Into the orchard where king and council were.
So they begin to plot the treacherous snare.

AOI

39

"Guènes, fair sir," said Marsile, "I allow,
Something too lightly I treated you just now
When in my fury I would have struck you down;
But by these pelts of sable fur I vow,
Which of good gold are worth five hundred pounds,
Richly I'll quite you ere the next day be out."
"This I refuse not", said Ganelon the Count;
"God, if He please, shall balance the account."

AOI

40

"Truly, Count Guènes," then said the King Marsile.
"I have in mind your right good friend to be.
Of Charlemayn fain would I hear you speak.
He's very old, a hard life his has been;
Two hundred years and more I know he's seen;
In lands so many his body he's fatigued,
Hard strokes so many he's taken on his shield,
Rich kings so many he's brought to beggary –
When will he weary of fighting in the field?"
"That's not his way", said Guènes, "in the least.
None knows the Emperor, or looks upon his mien,
But says of him: 'A right great man is he.'
Howe'er I sounded his praise and his esteem,
His worth and honour would still outrun my theme.
His mighty valour who could proclaim in speech?

71

God kindled in him a courage so supreme,
He'd rather die than fail his knights at need."

AOI

41

The Paynim said: "I marvel in my thought,
At Charlemayn, that is so old and hoar!
I know he's lived two hundred years and more.
In lands so many his body he's forworn,
Sharp strokes so many of lance and spear has borne,
Rich kings so many beggared and brought to naught –
When will he weary of going to the wars?"
"Never", said Guènes, "while Roland still bears sword;
There's none so valiant beneath the heavens broad,
Oliver too, his friend, is a brave lord;
And the Twelve Peers whom Charles so much adores
Protect the vanward with knights a thousand score;
Charles is secure, he fears no man at all."

AOI

42

The Paynim said: "I marvel in my mind
At Charlemayn whose head is old and white.
Two hundred years, I know, have passed him by.
In lands so many he's conquered far and wide,
Lance-thrusts so many he's taken in the strife,
Rich kings so many brought to a beggar's plight –
When will he weary of going forth to fight?"
"Never", said Guènes, "while Roland sees the light;
'Twixt east and west his valour has no like,
Oliver too, his friend, is a brave knight;
And the twelve Peers, in whom the King delights,
With twenty thousand Frenchmen to vanward ride:
Charles is secure, he fears no man alive."

AOI

43

"Guènes, fair sir," then said the King directly,
"I have an army, you will not find a better,
Four hundred thousand good knights as I may reckon:
Can I give battle to Carlon and his Frenchmen?"
Guènes replies: "Not you, and so I tell you,
For of your Paynims the losses would be deadly.
Leave all this folly, come to your sober senses.
Send to the Emperor so huge a heap of treasure
That all the French will marvel at its splendour.
For twenty sureties, that you will likewise send him,
Back to fair France Charles will return contented,
Leaving behind a rear-guard to protect him.
With them, I warrant, will be Roland his nephew,
Oliver too, the valorous and gentle.
Dead are these Counts, if you will give me credit.
Carlon will see his great pride fall'n and ended;
He'll have no heart to fight with you from henceforth."

                                        AOI

44

"Guènes, fair sir," [the King Marsilion cries,]
"What must I do to bring Roland to die?"
"I'll tell you that", Count Ganelon replies.
"At Sizer Gate the King will have arrived,
Leaving a rear-guard to keep the pass behind.
There'll be his nephew Count Roland, the great knight,
Oliver too, on whom he most relies,
With twenty thousand good Frenchmen at their side.

L. 583 *Sizer Gate: Port de Sizer*, or *Sizre* (the spelling varies) – this is the
pass now called the Col de Cize, which cuts through the Pyrenees on the
road running from St-Jean-Pied-de-Port by way of Roncevaux to
Pampeluna, and forms the "Gate of Spain".

73

An hundred thousand send of your Paynim kind,
And these shall first engage the French in fight.
Of the French force the loss will not be light –
Yours will be slaughtered, and that I'll not disguise!
The like assault you'll launch a second time,
And, first or last, Roland will not get by.
You will have done a deed of arms full fine;
You'll ne'er again see war in all your life.

AOI

45

Whoso should smite the County Roland dead,
From Carlon's body then were the right hand reft;
The wondrous armies would dwindle off and melt,
Nor could Charles gather so great a host afresh;
Our fathers' land would thus find peace and rest."
When he heard this Marsile fell on his neck,
And straightway bad them unlock his treasure-chests.

AOI

46

Then said Marsile: "One thing alone remains:
There's no good bond where there is no good faith;
Give me your oath Count Roland to betray."
Guènes replies: "It shall be as you say."
Upon the relics of his good sword Murgleys
He sware the treason and sware his faith away.

AOI

L. 600 *Our fathers' land* – *Tere Majur* (*terram majorum*): the land of one's
ancestors, the Fatherland – i.e. France. The phrase is often put into the
mouths even of Saracen speakers, as though it were a proper name. (Some
editors translate it simply "the Great Land", *terram majorem.*)

47

There was a faldstool of ivory all wrought;
Marsile commands a volume to be brought
Of Termagant's and of Mahomet's law;
The Saracen of Spain thereon has sworn
That in the rear-guard Count Roland shall be sought;
If there he find him, he'll fight with his whole force,
And do his best to slay him once for all.
Guènes replies: "And may it so befall!"

                                        AOI

48

Lo, now! there comes a Paynim, Valdebron;
He stands before the King Marsilion,
And gaily laughing he says to Ganelon:
"Here, take my sword, a better blade is none.
A thousand mangons are in the hilt thereof;
'Tis yours, fair sir, for pure affection,
For help against Roland the champion,
If in the rear-guard we find him as we want."
Quoth Ganelon to him: "It shall be done."
They kiss each other the cheek and chin upon.

49

Thereafter comes a Paynim, Climborin,
And laughing gaily to Ganelon begins:
"Come, take my helm, I ne'er saw none so rich:
[Above the nasal a carbuncle there is.
Out of pure friendship I offer you this gift]
If against Roland you'll aid us by your wit

L. 610 *a volume* – the Koran? (see Introduction, p. 20).
L. 621 *mangons* – the *mangon* is a Saracen gold coin.

75

That we may bring a shameful death on him."
"It shall be done", quoth Ganelon to this;
They kissed each other upon the mouth and chin.

AOI

50

Then to the Count Queen Bramimonda spoke:
"Dearly, fair sir, I love you, by my troth,
My king so lauds you, and his vassals also.
This pair of owches on your wife I bestow,
Heavy with jacinth and amethyst and gold;
More worth are they than all the wealth of Rome,
The like of them your Emperor never owned."
He takes the jewels and thrusts them in his poke.

AOI

51

The King calls Malduit, the keeper of his treasure:
"King Carlon's gifts, have you yet got them ready?"
And he replies, "Yea, sire, in ample measure:
Sev'n hundred camels laden with precious metal,
And twenty sureties, the noblest under heaven."

AOI

52

Marsilion's hand on Guènes' shoulder lies;
He says to him: "You are both bold and wise.
Now by that faith which seems good in your eyes
Let not your heart turn back from our design.
Treasure I'll give you, a great and goodly pile,
Ten mule-loads gold, digged from Arabian mines;
No year shall pass but you shall have the like.

L. 637 *owches* – brooches? (see Note, p. 205).
L. 641 *poke* – pouch (see Note, p. 205).

Take now the keys of this great burg of mine,
Offer King Charles all its riches outright.
Make sure that Roland but in the rear-guard rides,
And if in pass or passage I him find
I'll give him battle right bitter to abide."
"I think", said Guènes, "that I am wasting time."
He mounts his horse and on his journey hies.

AOI

53

The Emperor now returns upon his way
And has arrived before the town of Gayne
(Count Roland took it and all its wall down-razed,
An hundred years thereafter it lay waste;)
And there the King for news of Guènes waits,
And for the tribute of the great land of Spain.
In the white dawn, at breaking of the day,
Into the camp the County Guènes came.

AOI

54

Early that day the Emperor leaves his bed.
Matins and mass the King has now heard said;
On the green grass he stood before his tent.
Roland was with him, brave Oliver as well,
Naimon the Duke and many another yet.
Then perjured Guènes the traitor comes to them
And starts to speak with cunning false pretence.
He tells the King: "To you (whom God defend!)
Of Saragossa the keys I here present.
I bring you also wealth to your heart's content,
And twenty sureties: see they be closely kept.

L. 679 *twenty sureties* – this is the last we hear of the hostages, whose ultimate fate is not mentioned.

The valiant king, Marsile, this message sends:
The Caliph's absence he prays you'll not resent.
Mine own eyes saw four hundred thousand men
In hauberk armed, some having laced their helms,
And girt with swords whose hilts were richly gemmed,
Attend him forth; to the sea-shore they went.
The faith of Christ they'd keep not, nor accept,
And for this cause they from Marsilion fled.
But ere they'd sailed four leagues, maybe, or less,
Black wind and storm and tempest on them fell;
They were all drowned; they'll ne'er be seen again.
Had he been living I would have had him fetched.
Now, as regards the Paynim King himself:
Believe me, sire, before a month is sped
He'll follow you to France, to your own realm.
There he'll receive the faith that you profess,
There with joined hands to you his fealty pledge,
And hold from you in fief the Spanish realm."
Then said the King: "The name of God be blest!
Well have you done: I shall reward you well."
Throughout the host a thousand trumpets swell,
The French strike camp, their goods on sumpters set;
Home to fair France behold them all addressed.

                                                    AOI

55

King Charlemayn has spoiled the Spanish borders,
He's taken castles, put cities to the slaughter;
Now the King says he has ended his warfare.
Home to fair France the Emperor turns his horses.

                    •   •   •

Pennon to lancehead Count Roland now has corded;

LL. 706–707 – The scribe has perhaps omitted a line or two here, mentioning
where Charlemagne and his army have got to. We learn from laisse 58 that
they have reached the entrance to the pass, at the foot of the Pyrenees.

High on a hillock he displays it abroad there.
In fields all round the French set up their quarters.
Through the wide valleys the Paynim hosts go forward,
[All fully armed,] accoutred in their corslets,
Their helms laced on, and their swords in the sword-belt,
Shields on their necks, and their lances well ordered.
High on the mountains in a thicket they've halted:
Four hundred thousand they wait there for the morning;
God! it is grievous that the French have no warning!

AOI

56

The day goes down, dark follows on the day.
The Emperor sleeps, the mighty Charlemayn.
He dreamed he stood in Sizer's lofty gate,
Holding in hand his ashen lance full great.
Count Ganelon takes hold of it, and shakes,
And with such fury he wrenches it and breaks
That high as heaven the flinders fly away.
Carlon sleeps on, he sleeps and does not wake.

57

After this dream he had another dream:
That in his chapel at Aix in France was he;
In his right arm a fierce bear set its teeth.
Forth from Ardennes he saw a leopard speed,
That with rash rage his very body seized.
Then from the hall ran in a greyhound fleet,
And came to Carlon by gallops and by leaps.
From the first brute it bit the right ear clean,
And to the leopard gives battle with great heat.

LL. 727 sqq. *a fierce bear*, etc.: the bear is presumably Ganelon, as in laisse
186; the leopard, Marsilion; the greyhound, Roland.

The French all say the fight is good to see,
But none can guess which shall the victor be.
Carlon sleeps on; he wakes not from his sleep.

AOI

58

The night is past and the clear dawn is showing.
[A thousand trumpets] are sounded for the hosting.
The Emperor rides full lordly in his going.
"Barons, my lords," quoth Charlemayn, "behold now
These lofty passes, these narrows winding closely –
Say, who shall have the rearguard now to hold them?"
Quoth Ganelon: "I name my nephew Roland;
You have no baron who can beat him for boldness."
When the King heard, a stern semblance he showed him:
"A fiend incarnate you are indeed", he told him;
"Malice hath ta'en possession of you wholly!
Who then should keep the vanguard of my progress?"
Quoth Ganelon: "Ogier the Dane I vote for;
You have no baron can do it with more prowess."

AOI

59

When Roland hears what he's appointed to,
He makes reply as knighthood bids him do:
"My noble stepsire, I owe you gratitude
That I'm assigned the rearguard at your suit.
Charles, King of France, the loss shall never rue
Of steed or palfrey thereby, I warrant you,
No saddle-beast, nor hinny neither mule,
Pack-horse nor sumpter thereby he shall not lose,

L. 748 *who then should keep the vanguard?* – i.e. in Roland's place, since he usually takes command there with the other peers (see LL. 547–8, 560–1).

Save first the sword have paid the reckoning due."
Quoth Ganelon: "I know it; you speak truth."

AOI

60

When Roland hears that to the rearward guard
His stepsire names him, he speaks in wrath of heart:
"Ah! coward wretch, foul felon, baseborn carle,
Didst think the glove would fall from out my grasp
As did the wand from thine, before King Charles?"

AOI

61

"Just Emperor," then besought Count Roland bold,
"From your right hand deliver me your bow;
No man, I swear, shall utter the reproach
That I allowed it to slip from out my hold
As did the wand that Ganelon let go."
The Emperor sits with his head bended low,
On cheek and chin he plucks his beard for woe,
He cannot help but let the tears o'erflow.

L. 765 *the wand* – the mention of the wand, here and in L. 770, seems to
be a lapse of memory on the poet's part. Actually (LL. 331-333) it was the
glove that Ganelon let fall.
L. 767. *your bow* – the use of a bow as the token of an appointment does
not seem to be very usual, nor is it clear why Charlemagne should have one
in his hand, since the bow was not reckoned as a "noble" weapon, except
for use in hunting. Later MSS substitute, or add, the more customary glove
or standard.

62

Straightway thereon comes Naimon to the King –
No better vassal in court did ever sit.
He says to him: "You've listened to all this;
The County Roland is angered to the quick;
The rear-guard now has been adjudged to him
And you've no baron can ever make him quit.
Give him the bow now bended in your grip,
And find good men to aid him in this shift."
So the King gives it, and Roland seizes it.

63

To Roland then the King his uncle said:
"Nephew, fair sir, hear now and heed me well:
Half of my army I'll leave you for this stead;
Keep them with you and you'll be safe with them."
The Count said: "No; I never will consent;
May God confound me if I shame my descent!
A thousand score I'll keep of valiant French.
Safe through the passes go you with confidence;
Never fear man so long as I draw breath."

AOI

64

Roland the Count mounts on his destrier.
Comes then to him his comrade Oliver,
And Gerin comes and brave Count Gerier,
And Othon comes and so does Berenger,
Old Anseis, and Astor, great of worth,

And Gerard too, Roussillon's haughty earl;
And with them comes the rich Duke Gaïfer.
Quoth the Archbishop: "By Heav'n, I'm with you, sirs!"
"And so am I," Walter the Count affirms,
"I'm Roland's man, him am I bound to serve!"
Knights twenty thousand they choose for followers.

                                             AOI

65

To Walter Hum Count Roland gives command:
"A thousand French take, of our own French land,
And hold the gorges and heights on either hand;
Nor let the Emperor lose from his side one man."
Quoth Walter: "Mine to do as you demand."
With thousand French of France their own dear land
On gorge and hill Count Walter holds the flanks;
Come what come may he'll never quit his stand
Till from the sheath have flashed sev'n hundred brands.
King Almeric, lord of Balferna's strand,
That day shall give hard battle to their band.

66

High are the hills, the valleys dark and deep,
Grisly the rocks, and wondrous grim the steeps.
The French pass through that day with pain and grief;
The bruit of them was heard full fifteen leagues.
But when at length their fathers' land they see,

L. 797 *Gerard of Roussillon* – not Roussillon in the Pyrenees, but a hill in
Burgundy (now Mont Lassois), near the Abbey of Pothières, which was
founded, together with the Abbey of Vézelay by the historical Gerard.
His exploits are celebrated in the *Chanson de Geste* which bears his name.
L. 801 *man* – i.e. vassal.
L. 812. The engagement between Almeric and Walter Hum is not described
in the poem; its results are mentioned in laisse 152.

Their own lord's land, the land of Gascony,
Then they remember their honours and their fiefs,
Sweethearts and wives whom they are fain to greet,
Not one there is for pity doth not weep.
Charles most of all a boding sorrow feels,
His nephew's left the Spanish gates to keep;
For very ruth he cannot choose but weep.

AOI

67

All the twelve peers in Spain are left behind,
Full twenty thousand stout Frenchmen at their side;
Valiant they are, and have no fear to die.
To land of France the Emperor homeward hies.
And still his face beneath his cloak he hides.
Close at his rein the good Duke Naimon rides;
He asks the King: "What troubles thus your mind?"
"This is ill done", quoth Charles, "to ask me why!
So much I grieve I cannot choose but sigh.
Through Ganelon fair France is ruined quite.
An angel showed me a vision in the night,
How in my hand he broke my lance outright,
He that my nephew to the rear-guard assigned.
In foreign marches abandoned, Roland bides –
God! if I lose him I shall not find his like."

AOI

68

King Charlemayn from tears cannot refrain;
Full hundred thousand, the French grieve for his sake,
And for Count Roland are wondrously afraid.
Him has the false lord Ganelon betrayed;
Vast the reward the paynim king has paid:

L. 839 marches – the frontier region of a province; the province itself.

Silver and gold, and cloth of silk and saye,
Horses and mules, camels and beasts of prey.
Marsile has called the barony of Spain;
His viscounts, counts, almanzors stand arrayed,
Dukes and emirs, and youths of high estate;
Four hundred thousand he's summoned in three days.
In Saragossa he bids his tabors play;
Mahound their idol high on the tower they raise,
And every Paynim adores and gives it praise.
Then by forced marches their army hastes away,
Through Terracerta they ride by hill and dale.
Now have they seen French gonfalons displayed.
The twelve companions who in the rear-guard wait
Mean to give battle, and none shall say them nay.

69

Marsilion's nephew trips out before the throng,
Riding a mule which he whips with a wand;
He tells his uncle with laughter on his tongue:
"Fair sir and king, I've served you well and long;
Much have I suffered, much labour undergone,
Many fields fought, and many battles won!
First blow at Roland is the reward I want;
With my sharp sword I'll split him through the sconce!
Yea, if I find good favour with Mahond,
I'll set Spain free, unloosing of her bonds

L. 846 *saye* – a fine cloth of silk and wool.
L. 856 *Terracerta* – Tere Certaine – possibly Cerdagne, the region about
Catalonia.
L. 860 *Marsilion's nephew* – his name, as we learn in L. 1188, is Adelroth.
L. 866 *first blow at Roland* (*le colp de Roland*) – the privilege of striking the
first blow in the battle was much sought after. In L. 3200 we find Malpramis,
the son of the Emir Baligant, similarly demanding of his father the honour
(*le colp*) in the battle with Charlemagne. The commander-in-chief bestows
the honour by handing over his glove in token (L. 873).

From Gate of Spain to Durstant and beyond.
Charles will lose heart, the French will yield anon,
You shall be quit of wars your whole life long."
He gets the glove from King Marsilion.

AOI

70

Marsilion's nephew holds the glove in his fist:
Unto his uncle thus proudly he begins:
"Fair sire and king, you've made me a great gift.
Find me twelve lords, the best that you can pick.
'Gainst the twelve peers our valour for to pit."
The first that answers is Falsaron to wit,
He was own brother unto Marsile the king:
"You and I, nephew, will gladly go to it.
In very deed this battle will we give
To Carlon's rearward that guards his host for him:
The thing is done! by us they'll all be killed."

AOI

71

King Corsablis now springs from out the host,
Barbarian born, the magic art he knows.
Like a brave man thus valiantly he spoke:
"No coward I, no, not for all God's gold!"

. . .

Malprimis of Brigale comes spurring bold,
He'll run afoot swifter than steed can go;
With a loud voice before Marsile he boasts:
"I'll bear my body with you to Roncevaux:
If I find Roland I'll fight till he's laid low."

L. 888-9 A few lines seem to have been omitted here, completing Corsablis'
speech of defiance.

72

From Balaguet there cometh an Emir;
His form is noble, his eyes are bold and clear,
When on his horse he's mounted in career
He bears him bravely armed in his battle-gear,
And for his courage he's famous far and near;
Were he but Christian, right knightly he'd appear.
Before Marsile he cries for all to hear:
"To Roncevaux", saith he, "my course I'll steer;
If I find Roland, then death shall be his weird,
And Oliver's, and all of the Twelve Peers!
The French shall die the death in shame and tears.
King Charlemayn, the dotard old and blear,
Will soon be sick of waging warfare here!
Spain shall be ours in peace this many a year!"
The King Marsile pours thanks into his ears.

AOI

73

Comes an Almanzor, a lord of Moriane,
There's no worse villain in all the land of Spain.
Before Marsilion his bragging boast he makes:
"To Roncevaux I'll lead my people straight,
Full twenty thousand with spear and lance arrayed.
If I meet Roland I'll kill him, by my faith!
No day shall dawn but Carlon shall bewail."

AOI

74

And next there comes Turgis of Tortelosa;
A count he is, and the whole city owneth;
A right ill will to Christian men he showeth.

l. 902 *weird* – doom.

Before Marsile with the rest he enrols him.
He tells the King: "Fear not for any foeman!
Mahound's worth more than St Peter the Roman;
Serve him; the field is ours and ours the trophy!
To Roncevaux I go to meet with Roland;
There shall he die; he shall have help of no man.
See here my sword, how long it is and noble;
'Gainst Durendal I'll measure it right boldly;
Which shall prevail you'll not be long in knowing.
The French shall die if they dare to oppose us;
Carlon the old shall be grieving and groaning;
Crown nevermore shall he wear from that moment."

75

And Escremiz of Valterne is the next;
He owns that fief, and he's a Saracen;
Before Marsile he shouts amid the press:
"To Ronceval I go to stoop their crests.
If I find Roland, there shall he lose his head,
And Oliver, who's captain of the rest;
The whole Twelve Peers are all marked out for death.
The French shall die and France shall be bereft.
Few men of worth to Carlon shall be left."

AOI

76

Next comes a Paynim, called Estorgan by name,
Estramarin his comrade with him came;
Foul felons both and knavish traitors they.
Then said Marsile: "My lords, draw near, I pray;
Through Roncevaux you mean to force your way,
And lead my troops, and lend us your best aid."
And they reply: "Command, and we obey.

Both Oliver and Roland we'll assail,
Of the Twelve Peers none shall survive the fray.
Sharp are our swords and goodly are the blades,
All in hot blood we'll dye them red this day;
The French shall die, and Carlon shall bewail.
A gift we'll make you of the home of their race;
Come with us, King, and see how goes the game,
And as a gift we'll give you Charlemayn."

77

Then comes at speed Margaris of Seville,
Who holds his land as far as Cazmarin.
Ladies all love him, so beautiful he is,
She that beholds him has a smile on her lips,
Will she or nill she, she laughs for very bliss,
And there's no Paynim his match for chivalry.
He joins the throng and cries unto the King
Loudest of all: "Never you fear a whit!
In Roncevaux this Roland I'll go kill,
Nor Oliver shall any longer live;
All the Twelve Peers we'll cut in little bits.
Lo! here my sword with golden pummel gilt!
Th' Emir of Primes gave it me for a gift,
I swear I'll dye it vermilion to the hilt.
The French shall die and France in shame shall sit.
Old greybeard Charles shall never live, I think,
One day but what he'll rage and weep for this.
France can be ours in a year if we will;
In Saint-Denis we'll eat and sleep our fill."
The Paynim King makes deep salaam to him.

AOI

L. 973 *Saint-Denis* – a town near Paris with a famous abbey, founded by
Dagobert in 626, the burial-place of the Kings of France.

78

And last there comes Chernubles of Munigre;
His unshorn hair hangs trailing to his feet.
He for his sport can shoulder if he please
More weight than four stout sumpter-mules can heave.
He dwells in regions wherein, so 'tis believed,
Sun never shines nor springs one blade of wheat,
No rain can fall, no dew is ever seen,
There, every stone is black as black can be,
And some folk say it's the abode of fiends.
Chernubles saith: "My sword's girt in the sheath;
In Roncevaux red blood shall dye it deep.
Should Roland cross my path, that doughty chief,
And I not smite him, never put faith in me!
To this my blade his Durendal shall yield,
The French shall die, and France be left bereaved."
This said, the whole Twelve Champions are convened;
One hundred thousand stout Saracens they lead.
Each one afire with zeal to do great deeds.
Beneath a pine-grove they arm them for the field.

79

Now are the Paynims in Sarsen hauberks dight
Whereof the most with triple mail are lined;
Good Saragossa helms they lace on tight,
Swords of Viana steel gird on their thighs;
Spears of Valence they have, and shields full fine,
Their gonfalons are scarlet, blue, and white.
They leave their mules, their palfreys leave behind,
And mount their steeds; in serried ranks they ride.
Fair was the day, the sun shone clear and bright,
No piece of harness but glittered in the light.

A thousand trumpets ring out for more delight.
Great is the noise; it reaches the French lines.
Quoth Oliver: "I think, companion mine,
We'll need this day with Saracens to fight."
Roland replies: "I hope to God you're right!
Here must we stand to serve on the King's side.
Men for their lords great hardship must abide,
Fierce heat and cold endure in every clime,
Lose for his sake, if need be, skin and hide.
Look to it now! Let each man stoutly smite!
No shameful songs be sung for our despite!
Paynims are wrong, Christians are in the right!
Ill tales of me shall no man tell, say I!"

                                        AOI

80

Oliver's climbed upon a hilly crest,
Looks to his right along a grassy cleft,
And sees the Paynims and how they ride addressed.
To his companion Roland he calls and says:
"I see from Spain a tumult and a press –
Many bright hauberks, and many a shining helm!
A day of wrath, they'll make it for our French.
Ganelon knew it, false heart and traitor fell;
When to the Emperor he named us for this stead!"
Quoth Roland: "Silence, Count Oliver, my friend!
He is my stepsire, I will have no word said."

81

Oliver's climbed a hill above the plain,
Whence he can look on all the land of Spain,
And see how vast the Saracen array;
All those bright helms with gold and jewels gay,

And all those shields, those coats of burnished mail;
And all those lances from which the pennons wave;
Even their squadrons defy all estimate,
He cannot count them, their numbers are so great;
Stout as he is, he's mightily dismayed.
He hastens down as swiftly as he may,
Comes to the French and tells them all his tale.

82

Quoth Oliver: "The Paynim strength I've seen;
Never on earth has such a hosting been:
A hundred thousand in van ride under shield
Their helmets laced, their hauberks all agleam
Their spears upright, with heads of shining steel.
You'll have such battle as ne'er was fought on field.
My lords of France, God give you strength at need!
Save you stand fast, this field we cannot keep."
The French all say: "Foul shame it were to flee!
We're yours till death; no man of us will yield."

AOI

83

Quoth Oliver: "Huge are the Paynim hordes,
And of our French the numbers seem but small.
Companion Roland, I pray you sound your horn,
That Charles may hear and fetch back all his force."
Roland replies: "Madman were I and more,
And in fair France my fame would suffer scorn.
I'll smite great strokes with Durendal my sword,
I'll dye it red high as the hilt with gore.
This pass the Paynims reached on a luckless morn;
I swear to you death is their doom therefor."

AOI

84

"Companion Roland, your Olifant now sound!
King Charles will hear and turn his armies round;
He'll succour us with all his kingly power."
Roland replies: "May never God allow
That I should cast dishonour on my house
Or on fair France bring any ill renown!
Rather will I with Durendal strike out,
With this good sword, here on my baldrick bound;
From point to hilt you'll see the blood run down.
Woe worth the Paynims that e'er they made this rout!
I pledge my faith, we'll smite them dead on ground."

AOI

85

"Companion Roland, your Olifant now blow;
Charles in the passes will hear it as he goes,
Trust me, the French will all return right so."
"Now God forbid", Roland makes answer wroth,
"That living man should say he saw me go
Blowing of horns for any Paynim foe!
Ne'er shall my kindred be put to such reproach.
When I shall stand in this great clash of hosts
I'll strike a thousand and then sev'n hundred strokes,
Blood-red the steel of Durendal shall flow.
Stout are the French, they will do battle bold,
These men of Spain shall die and have no hope."

L. 1059 *Olifant* – the word (which is a form of "elephant") means (a) ivory,
(b) a horn made of ivory, and is used specifically, almost as a proper name,
to denote Roland's horn, made of an elephant's tusk, and adorned with
gold and jewels about the rim.

86

Quoth Oliver: "Herein I see no blame:
I have beheld the Saracens of Spain;
They cover all the mountains and the vales,
They spread across the hillsides and the plains;
Great is the might these foreigners display,
And ours appears a very small array."
"I thirst the more", quoth Roland, "for the fray.
God and His angels forbid it now, I pray,
That e'er by me fair France should be disfamed!
I'd rather die than thus be put to shame;
If the King loves us it's for our valour's sake."

87

Roland is fierce and Oliver is wise
And both for valour may bear away the prize.
Once horsed and armed the quarrel to decide,
For dread of death the field they'll never fly.
The counts are brave, their words are stern and high.
Now the false Paynims with wondrous fury ride.
Quoth Oliver: "Look, Roland, they're in sight.
Charles is far off, and these are very nigh;
You would not sound your Olifant for pride;
Had we the Emperor we should have been all right.
To Gate of Spain turn now and lift your eyes,
See for yourself the rear-guard's woeful plight.
Who fights this day will never more see fight."
Roland replies: "Speak no such foul despite!
Curst be the breast whose heart knows cowardise!
Here in our place we'll stand and here abide:
Buffets and blows be ours to take and strike!"

AOI

88

When Roland sees that battle there must be
Leopard nor lion ne'er grew so fierce as he.
He calls the French, bids Oliver give heed:
"Sir friend and comrade, such words you shall not speak!
When the King gave us the French to serve this need
These twenty thousand he chose to do the deed;
And well he knew not one would flinch or flee.
Men must endure much hardship for their liege,
And bear for him great cold and burning heat,
Suffer sharp wounds and let their bodies bleed.
Smite with your lance and I with my good steel,
My Durendal the Emperor gave to me:
And if I die, who gets it may agree
That he who bore it, a right good knight was he."

89

Then to their side comes the Archbishop Turpin,
Riding his horse and up the hillside spurring.
He calls the French and preaches them a sermon:
"Barons, my lords, Charles picked us for this purpose;
We must be ready to die in our King's service.
Christendom needs you, so help us to preserve it.
Battle you'll have, of that you may be certain,
Here come the Paynims – your own eyes have observed
    them.
Now beat your breasts and ask God for His mercy:
I will absolve you and set your souls in surety.
If you should die, blest martyrdom's your guerdon;
You'll sit on high in Paradise eternal."
The French alight and all kneel down in worship;

God's shrift and blessing the Archbishop conferreth,
And for their penance he bids them all strike firmly.

90

The French rise up and on their feet stand close;
All of their sins are shriven and made whole,
And the Archbishop God's blessing has bestowed.
Then on swift steeds they leap to saddlebow.
Armed with the arms prescribed by knightly code;
All are now ready into the field to go.
Count Roland said to Oliver right so:
"Sir my companion, too true the word you spoke,
That all of us by Ganelon were sold.
He's ta'en his wage of wealth and goods and gold.
The Emperor's vengeance I think will not be slow!
Marsile the King has bargained for our bones:
He'll need the sword to fetch his purchase home."

AOI

91

Through Gate of Spain Roland goes riding past
On Veillantif, his swiftly-running barb;
Well it becomes him to go equipped in arms,
Bravely he goes, and tosses up his lance,
High in the sky he lifts the lancehead far,
A milk-white pennon is fixed above the shaft
Whose falling fringes whip his hands on the haft.
Nobly he bears him, with open face he laughs;
And his companion behind him follows hard;
The Frenchmen all acclaim him their strong guard.
On Saracens he throws a haughty glance
But meek and mild looks on the men of France,
To whom he speaks out of a courteous heart:

"Now, my lord barons, at walking pace – advance!
Looking for trouble these Paynims ride at large –
A fine rich booty we'll have ere this day's past;
Never French king beheld the like by half."
E'en as he speaks, their battles join and charge.

AOI

92

Quoth Oliver: "I have no more to say:
To sound your horn for help you would not deign,
So here you are, you've not got Charlemayn;
Little he knows, brave heart! he's not to blame.
Nor those with him, nowise in fault are they.
Ride forward then and do the best you may!
Barons my lords, hold firm amid the fray!
Now for God's sake be resolute, I pray,
To strike hard blows, to give them and to take.
King Carlon's war-cry forget not to proclaim!"
A mighty shout the Frenchmen give straightway;
Whoso had heard the cry "Mountjoy" they raise
He would remember its valiance all his days.
They charge – Lord God, was ever sight so brave?
They spur their steeds to make the greater haste,
They fall afighting – there is no other way –
The Saracens join battle undismayed;
Paynims and Franks are fighting face to face.

L. 1181 *Mountjoy* – a mountjoy (montjoie) was (according to Littré) a
mound or cairn of stones set up to mark the site of a victory. The old French
war-cry, "Montjoie St-Denis!" or, briefly, "Montjoie!" derived from the
cairn set up at Saint-Denis on the site of the saint's martyrdom (his spiritual
victory). Others derive "Montjoie" from the Hill of Rama, called "Mons
Gaudii," from which pilgrims obtained their first view of Jerusalem.

93

Now Adelroth, (he was King Marsile's nephew),
Before the host comes first of all his fellows;
With evil words the French he thus addresses:
"Villainous Franks, with us you have to reckon!
You've been betrayed by him that should protect you,
Your king lacked wit who in the passes left you.
Fair France will lose her honour in this venture;
From Carlon's body the right arm will be severed."
When Roland hears him, God! but his rage is reckless!
He spurs his horse, gives full rein to his mettle,
His blow he launches with all his mightiest effort;
The shield he shatters, and the hauberk he rendeth,
He splits the breast and batters in the breast-bone,
Through the man's back drives out the backbone bended,
And soul and all forth on the spear-point fetches;
Clean through he thrusts him, forth of the saddle wrenching,
And flings him dead a lance-length from his destrier;
Into two pieces he has broken his neckbone.
No less for that he speaks to him and tells him:
"Out on thee, churl! no lack-wit is the Emperor,
He is none such, nor loved he treason ever;
Right well he did who in the passes left us,
Neither shall France lose honour by this venture.
First blood to us! Go to it, gallant Frenchmen!
Right's on our side, and wrong is with these wretches!"

AOI

94

A duke was there, he was named Falsaron,
Brother was he to King Marsilion,
Abiram's land and Dathan's did he own;
Under the sky was no worse villain known;

Between the eyes his brow was broad of bone,
A full half-foot it measured, I suppose.
His nephew's death he bitterly bemoans;
Forth of the press he gallops out alone,
The Paynim war-cry he utters as he goes,
And on the French an evil taunt bestows:
"Fair France this day shall find her honour flown!"
Oliver's heard him, great wrath within him grows,
Into his horse he strikes his spurs of gold,
Right baronly he rides to smite the foe.
He breaks the shield, he cleaves the hauberk close,
Clean through his breast drives lance and pennon both,
A spear's-length flings him dead from the saddle-bow;
Looks down and sees the infidel lie low
And thus upbraids him in a right haughty tone:
"Churl, for your threats I do not care a groat!
French lords, strike on! we'll have them all o'erthrown."
King Carlon's war-cry, "Mountjoy!" he shouts full bold.

AOI

95

A king was there, his name was Corsablis,
From a far land he came, from Barbary;
The Saracens he calls, and thus he speaks:
"Well are we placed this field of arms to keep;
For of these Franks the number is but weak,
And we may well despise the few we see.
Charles cannot come to help them in their need,
This is the day their deaths are all decreed!"
Archbishop Turpin has listened to his speech,
And hates him worse than any man that breathes.
His golden spurs he strikes into his steed,
And rides against him right valiant for the deed.
He breaks the buckler, he's split the hauberk's steel,

Into his breast driven the lance-head deep,
He spits him through, on high his body heaves,
And hurls him dead a spear's length o'er the lea.
Earthward he looks and sees him at his feet,
But yet to chide him he none the less proceeds:
"Vile infidel, you lied between your teeth!
Charles my good lord to help us will not cease,
Nor have our French the least desire to flee.
These friends of yours stock-still we're like to leave;
Here's news for you – you'll die, and there you'll be.
Frenchmen, strike home! forget not your high breed!
This first good stroke is ours, God's gramercy!"
He shouts "Mountjoy!" to hearten all the field.

96

And Gerin strikes Malprimis of Brigale;
No penny-piece the stubborn shield avails;
The crystal boss he splinters all in twain,
That half the buckler falls down upon the plain:
Through to the flesh he cleaves the hauberk-mail,
Through to the heart he drives the good spear straight;
The Paynim falls flat down with all his weight.
Then Satan comes and hales his soul away.

AOI

97

Gerier his friend on the Emir runs in,
Shatters the shield and bursts the byrny-rings,
Clean through the guts the trusty spear he swings,
Thrusts it well in, then out at back with it;
A whole spear's length on field the body flings:
Quoth Oliver: "We're doing well with this!"

98

Samson the Duke on the Almanzor runs:
Through gilded shield and painted flowers he thrusts;
Nought for defence avails the hauberk tough,
He splits his heart, his liver, and his lung,
And strikes him dead, weep any or weep none.
Cries the Archbishop: "This feat was knightly done!"

99

And Anseïs gives rein to his good steed,
He runs on Turgis of Tortelose at speed;
Under the boss of gold he cleaves the shield,
And of the hauberk the double mail unseams,
Into his body strikes home the head of steel,
Through to his back he drives the point out clean,
A full spear's length he flings him dead on field.
Quoth Roland: "Lo! that was a valiant feat!"

100

And Engelier the Gascon of Bordeaux
Spurs his good steed, slacks rein and lets him go;
With Escrimiz, Valterna's lord, he's closed,
Off from his neck the splintered buckler broke.
The hauberk's ventail he's shattered with the stroke.
He splits his throat between the collar-bones,
A full spear's length dead from the saddle throws;
Then says to him: "The devil take thy soul!"

AOI

101

101

And Othon strikes a Paynim, Estorgant,
Full in mid-chief he smites the shield point-blank,
So that the white splits and the scarlet cracks;
The skirt of mail he's riven through and smashed,
Into his body the cleaving spear he rams;
From his swift steed he hurls him dead on land,
"And now", says he, "find comfort if you can!"

102

Then Berenger drives at Estramarin,
He cleaves the shield, and the good hauberk splits,
On his stout spear the trunk of him he spits
And flings him dead 'mid thousand Sarrasins.
Of the Twelve Peers ten are already killed,
Two and no more are left of them who live;
These are Chernubles and the Count Margaris.

103

Now Margaris is a right valiant peer,
Buxom and strong, nimble and fleet and fierce.
He spurs his horse to strike at Olivere;
He splits the shield, the golden boss he sheers,
Along his ribs the glancing spear-point veers,
But by God's grace his body is not pierced;
Nor is he thrown, though the shock breaks the spear.
Past him the Paynim is borne in full career,
Rallying his men he sounds his bugle clear.

L. 1308 *the Twelve Peers* – i.e. the Saracen Peers enumerated in LL. 878–990.

104

Great is the battle and crowded the mellay,
Nor does Count Roland stint of his strokes this day;
While the shaft holds he wields his spear amain –
Fifteen great blows ere it splinters and breaks.
Then his bare brand, his Durendal, he takes;
Against Chernubles he spurs his steed in haste,
Splits through the helm with carbuncles ablaze,
Through the steel coif, and through scalp and through brain
'Twixt the two eyes he cleaves him through the face;
Through the bright byrny close-set with rings of mail,
Right through the body, through the fork and the reins,
Down through the saddle with its beaten gold plates,
Through to the horse he drives the cleaving blade,
Seeking no joint through the chine carves his way,
Flings horse and man dead on the grassy plain.
"Foul befal, felon, that e'er you sought this fray!
Mahound", quoth he, "shall never bring you aid.
Villains like you seek victory in vain."

105

The County Roland throughout the field goes riding;
With Durendal, good sword, he stabs and slices,
The toll he takes of Saracens is frightful.
Would you had seen him, dead man on dead man piling,
Seen the bright blood about his pathway lying!
Bloody his hauberk and both his arms with fighting,
His good horse bloody from crest to withers likewise;
Oliver too doth never cease from striking,
And the Twelve Peers are not a whit behindhand,
And all the French are hammering and smiting;
The Paynims fall, some dead and others dying.

Quoth the Archbishop: "Right blessèd be our knighthood";
He shouts "Mountjoy!" war-cry of Charles the mighty.

AOI

106

And Oliver goes riding through the press;
His spear is broken, only the shaft is left.
Against a Paynim, Malun, he rides addrest,
Smashes the shield with flowers and gold bedecked,
Both of his eyes he smites out of his head,
So that his brains around his feet are spread,
And flings the corpse amid sev'n hundred dead.
Turgis he's slain, and slain Esturgot next,
Till to the grips the spear-shaft splits in shreds.
Roland cries out: "What are you doing, friend?
I'd give no groat for sticks in such a stead!
Here iron avails, and steel and nothing else.
Where is your sword that Hauteclaire is y-clept,
With its gold hilts and pummel crystal-gemmed?"
"I've had no time to draw," Oliver said,
"I've been so busy with striking right and left."

AOI

107

Dan Oliver has drawn his goodly brand,
As his friend Roland so urgently demands;
Now will he prove him a stout knight of his hands!
He smites a Paynim, Justin of Val Ferrat;
Clean through the middle the skull of him he cracks,
The saffron byrny splits, and his breast and back,

L. 1363 *y-clept* – named.
L. 1367 *Dan* (Dominus) – lord.
L. 1372 *saffron* – burnished with a yellow varnish made from bismuth oxide.

And saddle, brave with gems and golden bands,
And through the spine the horse in sunder hacks,
And dead on field flings all before him flat.
"I'll call you brother," quoth Roland, "after that!
'Tis for such strokes our Emperor loves a man."
The shout "Mountjoy!" goes up on every hand.

AOI

108

Gerin the Count bestrides his steed Sorel,
Gerier his comrade on Passëcerf is set;
Eagerly both loose rein and spur ahead
And go to strike a Paynim, Timozel,
One on the shield, the other on the chest.
Both spears at once are broken in his breast,
Flat in the fallow straightway they fling him dead –
I do not know, I never have heard tell,
Which of the two was the more swift and snell.
[And Engelier, Knight of Bordeaux, he next
Slew Esprevere, that son was to Burel.]
Archbishop Turpin has o'erthrown Siglorel,
The sorcerer, who'd once been down to Hell,
With Jupiter for guide, by magic spells.
Quoth Turpin then: "Ear-marked was he for death!"
Roland replies: "The churl has made an end.
Oliver, brother, such strokes delight me well!"

L. 1387 *snell* – speedy.
LL. 1388-1389 – these two lines have been telescoped in the text, and are
thus emended by most editors.
L. 1392 *Jupiter* – like Apollo, the classical Jove has been demoted to the
status of demon.

109

Fiercer and still more fierce the battle grows;
Both French and Paynims deal wondrous heavy strokes,
Some in attacking, and some in parrying blows.
How many spears are bloodied there and broke!
What gonfalons, what banners rent and strown!
How many French in flower of youth laid low,
Whom wives and mothers shall never more behold,
Nor those of France who wait them on the road!
King Charlemayn must weep and wail for woe;
What help in that? he cannot save his folk.
Ill did Count Guènes serve Carlon, when he rode
To Saragossa and all his people sold;
Thereby he lost life and limbs of his own
When at Aix after they judged him to the rope,
And of his kin thirty were hanged also,
Who ne'er had thought such death should be their dole.

AOI

110

Fierce is the battle and wondrous grim the fight.
Both Oliver and Roland boldly smite,
Thousands of strokes the stout Archbishop strikes,
The whole Twelve Peers are not a whit behind,
And the French ranks lay on with all their might.
Heaped by the hundred thousands of Paynims lie,
None can escape unless he turns and flies,
Will he or nill he, there must he leave his life.
There France must lose the noblest of her knights,
They'll see no more their kindred and their sires,
Nor Charles, who scans the pass with anxious eyes.

L. 1409 *to the rope* – so in L. 3932, but in the event, a much more horrible
death is meted out to Ganelon (LL. 3963 sqq).

Throughout all France terrific tempests rise,
Thunder is heard, the stormy winds blow high,
Unmeasured rain and hail fall from the sky,
While thick and fast flashes the levin bright,
And true it is the earth quakes far and wide.
Far as from Saintes to Michael-of-the-Tide,
From Besançon to Wissant Port, you'd find
There's not a house but the walls crack and rive.
Right at high noon a darkness falls like night,
Save for the lightning there's not a gleam of light;
None that beholds it but is dismayed for fright,
And many say: "This is the latter time,
The world is ending, and the Great Doom is nigh."
They speak not true, they cannot read the signs:
'Tis Roland's death calls forth this mighty cry.

III

The French have fought with valour and success;
By scores and thousands lie Paynim corpses spread,
Of hundred thousand scarce two will fight again.
Quoth the Archbishop: "Right valiant are our men,
The like of these hath no lord under heav'n.
Thus it is written in the Gestes of the French:
Our Emperor's power was never rivalled yet."
They search the field for their maimed and their dead,
With grief and sorrow the eyes of them are wet,
With love and pity for their kindred and friends.
Now falls upon them Marsile with all his strength.

                                         AOI

L. 1443 *The Gestes of the French* – the chronicle, to which the poet from
time to time refers, and from which he claims to derive his information.

112

The King Marsile comes riding up a gorge
With all his army about him in great force;
He has assembled twenty huge battle-hordes.
Such flash of helms with gems and gold adorned!
Such shields, such byrnies with burnished saffron wrought!
Sev'n hundred trumpets are sounding the assault;
Through all the country the noise of them goes forth.
"Brother," quoth Roland, "friend Oliver, sweet lord,
It is our death false Ganelon has sworn;
The treason's plain, it can be hid no more;
A right great vengeance the Emperor will let fall.
But we must bide a fearful pass of war.
No man has ever beheld the like before.
I shall lay on with Durendal my sword,
You, comrade, wield that great Hauteclaire of yours.
In lands how many have we those weapons borne!
Battles how many victoriously fought!
Ne'er shall base ballad be sung of them in hall!"

AOI

113

Marsile beholds his slaughtered chivalry.
He bids his trumpets and horns sound instantly
And then sets forward with his great company.
Then first rides out a Saracen, Abisme,
In all that host was none more vile than he,
With evil vice and crimes he's dyed full deep,
In Mary's Child, God's Son, he's no belief,
And black he is as melted pitch to see.
Better he loves murder and treachery
Than all the gold that is in Galicie
None ever saw him in mirth or jollity;

But bold he is and rash to a degree,
And for that reason he's loved by King Marsile.
He bears a dragon to rally his meinie.
The good Archbishop observes him, much displeased,
He'd like to hit him on sight, that's how he feels,
And to himself he says quite quietly:
"This Sarsen looks right heretic to me.
'Twere best by far to go and kill the beast;
I never loved cowards nor coward deeds."

AOI

114

Th'Archbishop opens the battle up anew;
He rides a charger that from Grossayle he took
(That was a king in Denmark, whom he slew).
A steed he is swiftly-running and smooth,
Flat in the knee and hollow in the hoof,
Short in the thigh and ample in the croup,
Long in the flank and the back well set up,
White of his tail and yellow of his plume,
Small of his ears and his head tawny-hued;
Here is a horse no courser could outdo.
Him the Archbishop, of his valour right good,
Spurs on Abisme, and none shall stay his mood.
He rides to strike him on his target of proof
Wondrous with topaz and amethyst to boot,
With carbuncle ablaze, and beryl blue
(Emir Galafe gave it him for a boon
Whom in Val Metas a devil gave it to.)
Turpin lays on, nor spares; I tell you true,

L. 1480 *meinie* – household.
LL. 1491–1495 – with this classic enumeration of the good points of a horse compare Shakespeare, *Venus and Adonis* 295–298. The two descriptions have much in common, except that the mediaeval writer attaches much more importance to colour.

After he hit it it was not worth a sou!
From flank to flank he spits his body through,
And flings him dead wherever he finds room.
The French all cry: "A valiant blow and shrewd!
Right strong to save is our Archbishop's crook!"

115

Now can the French count up the Paynim might
They see it filling the plains from side to side.
They urge on Roland and Oliver likewise
And the Twelve Peers to flee for all their lives;
To whom straightway the Prelate speaks his mind:
"Barons, my lords, these shameful thoughts put by;
By God I charge you, hold fast and do not fly,
Lest brave men sing ill songs in your despite.
Better it were to perish in the fight.
Soon, very soon we all are marked to die,
None of us here will see to-morrow's light;
One thing there is I promise you outright:
To you stand open the gates of Paradise,
There with the holy sweet Innocents to bide."
His words so fill them with courage and delight
There's none among them but shouts "Mountjoy" on high.
                                                    AOI

116

A Saracen, of Saragossa Town
Was there, the lord of half that city round –
Climborin namely, that traitor false and foul
Which took the oath of Ganelon the Count
And then for friendship kissed him upon the mouth
And with his helm and carbuncle endowed;
Our Fatherland he swore he'd disrenown,

And from the Emperor would snatch away the crown.
Now he comes riding on Barbēmouche his mount –
Fleeter was never swallow nor falcon found –
Slacks rein, spurs hard its mettle to arouse,
On Engelier the Gascon forward bounds.
Buckler nor byrny avails against him now,
Into the midriff lance-point and pennon plough,
From breast to back the shaft runs through and out,
A whole spear's length he hurls him dead on ground.
"Fit for destruction is all this gear!" he shouts;
"Paynims, strike hard! carve your way through the rout!"
"God!" say the French, "one of our best is down!"

AOI

117

Count Roland calls to Oliver his friend:
"Fair sir, companion, see, Engelier is dead;
No better man had we for knightliness."
The Count replies: "God give me fair revenge!"
In his steed's flanks the golden spurs he sets,
He grasps Hauteclaire, whose steel is all dyed red,
He deals the Paynim a mighty stroke and dread,
Twists out the blade, down falls the Saracen;
The Adversary bears off his soul to Hell.
Then he goes on, slays Duke Alfayen next,
From Escababa he hews away the head,
And seven Arabs unhorses then pell-mell:
That lot at least will never fight again.
"My friend is angry", the County Roland said:
"Fighter for fighter he matches me right well;
'Tis for such strokes King Carlon loves us best!"
Aloud he cries: "Strike on, my valiant men!"

AOI

L. 1553 *the Adversary* – i.e. Satan.

118

Elsewhere, behold a Paynim, Valdabron,
Was godfather to King Marsilion;
He owns a navy four hundred dromonds strong,
And to his service no seaman but is bond.
He captured Salem by fraud in times bygone,
And sacked the Temple of good King Solomon,
Murdering there the Patriarch by the font.
He took the oath of County Ganelon,
And sword and mangons gave him as pledge thereon.
He rides a horse that he calls Gramimond,
Never of speed was peregrine more prompt.
With the sharp spur he urges it headlong;
The great Duke Samson straightway he falls upon.
He splits the shield, he bursts the habergeon,
Drives through his body spear-head and gonfalon,
Flings him from saddle a full spear's length along:
"Paynims!" he cries, "we'll beat them yet! Lay on!"
"God!" say the French, "there's a brave baron gone!"
                                                    AOI

119

When the Count Roland sees Samson thus laid low
Well may you guess how he is grieved of soul.
He spurs his horse and speeds to smite the foe
With Durendal, more worth than finest gold.
By might and main the Baron deals the stroke
Full on the helm that is all gemmed with gold;
The skull he splits, byrny and breast are broke,
Cloven the saddle, that is all gemmed with gold;
Through the beast's back deep down the weapon goes;

L. 1564 *dromond(s)* – a large and very swift mediaeval sailing-ship, used
both for war and commerce.

Like it or leave it, he has destroyed them both.
The Paynims say: "This is a bitter blow!"
"I love you not," quoth Roland, "by my troth;
Yours is the outrage, yours is the lying boast!"

AOI

120

An African there was of Afric, too,
Was called Malquiant, the son of King Malcude;
Harnessed he is in gold from head to foot,
None in the sun so glitters to the view,
He rides a horse that he calls Saut-Perdu;
No steed could rival the swiftness of its hoofs.
He strikes Anseïs in mid-shield square and true,
He shears away the scarlet and the blue,
Rips the mailed skirt of the hauberk of proof,
Into the body drives the steel and the wood.
The Count falls dead, his days have met their doom.
The French all say: "Brave lord, alack for you!"

121

Archbishop Turpin goes riding through the field;
Ne'er was mass sung by any tonsured priest
That of his body could do such valiant deeds!
He hails the Paynim: "God send the worst to thee!
Thou hast slain one for whom my whole heart grieves."
Into a gallop he urges his good steed,
He strikes him hard on his Toledo shield,
And lays him dead upon the grassy green.

122

There was a Paynim, and Grandoyne was he called,
King Capuel's son, from Cappadocia's shores,
Mounted on Marmor, for so he names his horse,
Swifter of speed than any bird that soars.
He slacks the rein and he goes spurring forth,
And runs to strike Gerin with all his force.
From off his neck he splits the red shield shorn,
From off his body he rips the byrny torn,
Into his heart the pennon blue he's borne,
And down he flings him dead on a rocky tor.
Gerin his comrade he smites down afterward,
Berenger next, Guy of St Antoine fall;
And then he strikes the mighty duke Astorge,
(Envers-on-Rhône and Valence called him lord),
And lays him dead; for joy the Paynims roar;
The French all say: "What loss we have to mourn!"

AOI

123

The County Roland grips fast his blood-red blade;
Well has he heard how the French are dismayed;
His heart grieves so, 'tis like to split in twain.
In hails the Paynim: "God send thee all His plagues!
Thou hast slain one for whom I'll make thee pay!"
He spurs his horse that gladly runs apace;
Let win who may, they're at it, face to face.

AOI

124

The Prince Grandoyne was a good knight and gallant,
Strong of his hands and valorous in battle;
Athwart him now comes Roland the great captain;

114

He'd never met him, but he knew him instanter.
By his proud aspect, and by his noble stature,
His haughty looks, and his bearing and manner.
He cannot help it, a mortal fear unmans him;
Fain would he fly, but what's the good? he cannot.
The Count assails him with such ferocious valour
That to the nasal the whole helmet is shattered,
Cloven the nose and the teeth and the palate,
The jaz'rain hauberk and the breastbone and backbone,
Both silver bows from off the golden saddle;
Horseman and horse clean asunder he slashes,
Lifeless he leaves them and the pieces past patching.
The men of Spain fall a-wailing for sadness:
The French all cry: "What strokes! and what a champion!"

125

Fierce is the battle and marvellous and great.
The Frenchmen ply their burnished spears amain.
There had you seen how many men in pain,
How many wounded and bleeding there and slain!
Heaped up pell-mell they lie, on back or face.
The Saracens cannot endure the strain;
Will they or nill they they flee across the plain,
And the French forces with all their might give chase.

AOI

126

Wondrous the battle, and it grows faster yet;
The French fight on with rage and fury fell,
They lop off wrists, hew ribs and spines to shreds,
They cleave the harness through to the living flesh;
On the green ground the blood runs clear and red.

L. 1647 *jazerain* – a kind of chain-mail made in Algiers (Al-Djezair).

[The Paynims say: "We cannot stand the stress,]
French Fatherland, be curst of Máhomet!
Your sons are bravest of all the sons of men."
There's none of them but cries: "Marsile to help!
Ride, ride, O King, for we are hard bested."

127

Roland the Count calls out to Olivere:
"Fair sir, companion, confess that for this gear
Our lord Archbishop quits him like any peer;
Earth cannot match him beneath the heavens' sphere,
Well does he know to handle lance and spear."
The Count replies: "Let's aid him now and here!"
At this the French lay on the lustier,
Hard are their strokes, the fight is very fierce,
And for the Christians the losses are severe.
Who then had seen Roland and Olivere
Smite with their swords and through all the press pierce!
And the Archbishop goes thrusting with his spear.
Of those they slew the numbers are writ clear
In many charters and tales of chroniclers:
More than four thousand as in the Geste appears.
Four great assaults they've borne with right good cheer;
Then comes a fifth, doleful and dread and drear.
All the French knighthood has fallen in career;
Sixty alone by God's grace persevere;
These ere they die will sell their bodies dear.

AOI

128

When County Roland sees all his brave men down,
To Oliver his friend he cries aloud:
"For God's sake, comrade, fair sir, what think you now?

See what good knights lie here upon the ground!
Well may we pity this fair sweet France of ours,
Thus left so barren of all her knighthood's flower.
Why aren't you here, O friend and Emperour?
Oliver, brother, what way is to be found?
How send him news of what is come about?"
Oliver said: "And how should I know how?
I'd rather die than we should lose renown."

AOI

129

"I'll sound", quoth Roland, "my Olifant straightway;
When Carlon hears, passing through Gate of Spain,
I pledge my word, the French will turn again."
Quoth Oliver: "It would be foul disdain,
And to your kindred the reproach would be great:
All their lives long they'd not live down the shame.
When I desired you, why then you said me nay;
If now you do it, of me you'll get no praise.
Blow if you will – such conduct is not brave.
Nay, but how deep in blood your arms are bathed!"
The Count replies: "I've struck good blows this day."

AOI

130

Said Roland then: "Full grievous is this fight.
I'll sound my horn, and Charles will hear the cry."
Quoth Oliver: " 'Twould ill beseem a knight.
I asked you, comrade, and you refused, for pride.
Had Charles been here, then all would have gone right;
He's not to blame, nor the men at his side.
Now by my beard (quoth he) if e'er mine eyes
Again behold my sister Aude the bright,
Between her arms never you think to lie."   AOI

131

Quoth Roland: "Why so angry with me, friend?"
And he: "Companion, you got us in this mess.
There is wise valour, and there is recklessness:
Prudence is worth more than foolhardiness.
Through your o'erweening you have destroyed the French;
Ne'er shall we do service to Charles again.
Had you but given some heed to what I said,
My lord had come, the battle had gone well,
And King Marsile had been captured or dead.
Your prowess, Roland, is a curse on our heads.
No more from us will Charlemayn have help,
Whose like till Doomsday shall not be seen of men.
Now you will die, and fair France will be shent;
Our loyal friendship is here brought to an end;
A bitter parting we'll have ere this sun set."

AOI

132

When the Archbishop thus hears them in dispute,
With his gold spurs he pricks his steed anew,
Draws near to them and utters this rebuke:
"Lord Oliver, and you, Lord Roland, too,
Let's have no quarrel, o'God's name, 'twixt you two.
It will not save us to sound the horn, that's true;
Nevertheless, 'twere better so to do.
Let the King come; his vengeance will be rude;
None shall to Spain ride home with merry news.
After, our French will light them down on foot,
Seek out our bodies and limbs in sunder hewn,
Lay us on biers borne upon sumpter-mules,
And weep for us with grief right pitiful;

L. 1734 *shent* – put to shame.

In the church-close we shall have burial due,
And not be food for dogs and swine and wolves."
Quoth Roland, "Sir, your words are right and good."

                                        AOI

133

Roland has set Olifant to his lips,
Firmly he holds it and blows it with a will.
High are the mountains, the blast is long and shrill,
Thirty great leagues the sound went echoing.
King Carlon heard it and all who rode with him.
"Lo, now, our men are fighting", quoth the King.
Guènes retorts: "If any man said this
Except yourself, it were a lie, methinks."

                                        AOI

134

The County Roland with pain and anguish winds
His Olifant, and blows with all his might.
Blood from his mouth comes spurting scarlet-bright
He's burst the veins of his temples outright.
From hand and horn the call goes shrilling high:
King Carlon hears it who through the passes rides,
Duke Naimon hears, and all the French beside.
Quoth Charles: "I hear the horn of Roland cry!
He'd never sound it but in the thick of fight."
"There is no battle", Count Ganelon replies;
"You're growing old, your hair is sere and white,
When you speak thus, you're talking like a child.
Full well you know Roland's o'erweening pride;
'Tis strange that God endures him so long time!
Took he not Noples against your orders quite?
The Paynims made a sally from inside,
And there gave battle to Roland the great knight;

So he swilled down the field – a brave device
To keep the bloodstains from coming to your eyes!
For one small hare he'll blow from morn till night;
Now to the Peers he's showing-off in style.
Who dare attack him? No man beneath the sky!
Ride on, ride on! Why loiter here the while?
Our Fathers' land lies distant many a mile."

AOI

135

Count Roland's mouth with running blood is red;
He's burst asunder the temples of his head;
He sounds his horn in anguish and distress.
King Carlon hears, and so do all the French.
Then said the King: "This horn is long of breath."
"'Tis blown", quoth Naimon, "with all a brave man's
  strength;
Battle there is, and that I know full well.
He that would stay you is but a traitor fell.
To arms! let sound your battle-cry to heav'n!
Make haste to bring your gallant household help!
You hear how Roland makes desperate lament!"

136

The Emperor Charles lets sound his horns aloft.
The French light down and arm themselves anon
With helm and hauberk and gilded swords girt on;
Goodly their shields, their lances stiff and strong,
Scarlet and white and blue the gonfalons.
Straightway to horse the warrior lords have got;
Swift through the passes they spur and never stop.
Each unto other they speak and make response:
"Might we reach Roland ere he were dead and gone,

We'ld strike good strokes beside him in the throng."
What use is that? They have delayed too long.

137

Vespers draws on and shining is the day;
Against the sun glitters their armed array,
Hauberk and helm flash back a mighty blaze,
So many shields their painted flowers display,
Such store of spears with gilded pennons gay!
The Emperor rides right wrathful on his way.
And all the French in anger and dismay;
There is not one but weeps for very rage;
For Roland's sake they're grievously afraid.
The King arrests Count Ganelon straightway;
He's turned him over to the cooks in his train;
The master-cook he calls, Besgun by name:
"Guard me him well, as fits a man so base,
For all my house this villain has betrayed!"
Besgun takes charge, with five-score kitchen knaves,
The best and worst that serve in that estate.
They pluck the beard from off his chin and face,
With four sound thumps each gives him a good baste,
With sticks and faggots they pound him and they paste,
And round his neck they fasten a strong chain,
Right well they chain him like a bear in a cage;
Now on a pack-horse they've hoisted him in shame;
Till Carlon want him 'tis they will keep him safe.

AOI

138

Huge are the hills and shadowy and high,
Deep in the vales the living streams run by.
The trumpets sound before them and behind,
All with one voice to Olifant reply.
In wrath of heart the Emperor Carlon rides,
And all the French in sorrow and in ire;
There's none but grieves and weeps from out his eyes;
They all pray God to safeguard Roland's life
Till they may come to battle by his side;
Once they are with him they'll make it a great fight.
What use is that? their prayers are empty quite,
Too long they've lingered, they cannot come in time.

                                                    AOI

139

King Charlemayn rides on in anger grim,
Over his byrny flows the white beard of him;
All the French barons beside him spur full swift;
There's none of them but is with fury filled
Not to be aiding Roland the Paladin
Now that he's fighting the Spanish Sarrasins.
He's hurt so sore, I fear he cannot live.
God! and what men, those sixty with him still!
Better had never nor captain nor yet king.

                                                    AOI

140

Roland surveys the mountains and the fells;
How many French he sees there lying dead!
Like a good knight he makes them this lament:
"Barons, my lords, may God of His largesse
Bring all your souls to Paradise the blest,

Amid bright flowers to make their hallowed beds!
I never saw braver or truer men.
So long you served me unceasingly and well,
So many lands conquered for Carlon's realm!
The Emperor bred you alas! to what sad end!
O dearest land, fair nursery of the French,
By what hard hap art thou this day bereft!
Barons of France, for me you go to death,
Nought can I give you of safeguard or defence;
Now aid you God, who ne'er failed any yet!
Oliver, brother, you shall not lack my help.
Though none should slay me I'll die of grief no less;
Sweet sir, companion, let's go and fight afresh!"

141

The County Roland returns into the field
And like a warrior his Durendal he wields;
Faldron de Puy through the midriff he cleaves
With four-and-twenty besides, of great esteem.
Never on vengeance was any man so keen.
E'en as the deer before the deerhound flees
So before Roland the Paynims show their heels.
Quoth the Archbishop: "Well done, well done indeed!
Valour like this becomes a knight of breed
That bears his arms and sits a goodly steed;
Forward and fierce in battle should he be,
Else he's not worth a single penny-piece,
Best he turn monk in monastery meek
And for our sins pray daily on his knees."
Quoth Roland: "Strike, spare none of them," saith he.
At this the French renew the fight with speed;
Therein the Christians endure great loss and grief.

142

When it is known no prisoners will be made
Men fight back fiercely, and stubborn is the fray;
Therefore the French grow very lions for rage.
Here comes Marsile, e'en as a baron brave,
Riding a horse, and Gaignun is its name.
Full upon Bevon he rides and spurs amain,
That held all Beaune and Dijon for domain.
The shield he shatters, and the hauberk he breaks,
And lays him dead, he need not strike again.
And Ivon next and Ivor too, his mate,
And Gerard too of Roussillon he slays.
Roland the Count, who is not far away,
Cries to the Paynim: "God damn your soul, I say!
These my companions by treason you have slain!
Ere we go hence a bitter price you'll pay,
And you shall learn the name of my good blade!"
He rides to strike him, e'en as a baron brave;
From his sword-arm he shears the hand away.
And Jurfaret the Fair he next waylays,
Marsilion's son, and slices off his pate.
The Paynims cry: "Mahound! Mahound to aid!
Venge us on Carlon, all you gods of our faith!
Into our land he's sent this evil race!
Come life come death they'll never quit the place."
Then one to other cries: "Fly then! fly in haste!"
An hundred thousand have fled the field straightway;
They'll not return, call after them who may.

                                                    AOI

143

What help is that? Marsile has taken flight,
Yet there remains his uncle Marganice,
That governs Carthage, Alfrere and Garamile,
And Ethiope, a land accursed and vile.
In his command are all the Negro tribes;
Thick are their noses, their ears are very wide;
Full fifty thousand are gathered in their lines,
Boldly and fast and furiously they ride,
Yelling aloud the Paynim battle-cry.
Then Roland said: "Here are we doomed to die;
Full well I know we cannot long survive.
Fail not, for shame, right dear to sell your lives.
Lift up, my lords, your burnished blades and fight!
Come life, come death, the foe shall pay the price,
Lest we should bring fair France into despite!
When on this field Carlon my lord sets eyes
He'll see what toll we've taken of their might:
Fifteen dead Paynims for each of us he'll find;
Nor fail to bless us for this our great emprise."

AOI

144

When Roland looks on these accursed tribesmen –
As black as ink from head to foot their hides are,
With nothing white about them but their grinders –
Then said the Count: " 'Tis true beyond denial,
Right well I know it, this day shall death betide us.
I'll to the throng; Frenchmen, fight on beside me!"
Quoth Oliver: "The devil take the hindmost!"
The French hear this and once more fall a-fighting.

AOI

L. 1931 *emprise* – enterprise, feat of arms.

145

When Paynims see how few the French are grown
They plume themselves, puffed up with pride and hope:
"Now to the Emperor," they say, "his crimes come home!"
Marganice comes, riding a sorrel colt;
He spurs him hard with rowels all of gold,
And from behind deals Oliver a blow;
Deep in his back the burnished mail is broke,
That the spear's point stands forth at his breast-bone.
He saith to him: "You've suffered a sore stroke;
Charlemayn sent you to the pass for your woe.
Foul wrong he did us, 'tis good he lose his boast:
I've well requited our loss on you alone."

AOI

146

Oliver feels that he is hurt to death;
He grasps his sword Hauteclaire the keen of edge,
Smites Marganice on his high golden helm,
Shearing away the flowers and crystal gems,
Down to the teeth clean splits him through the head,
Shakes loose the blade and flings him down and dead;
Then saith: "Foul fall you, accursèd Paynim wretch!
Charles has had losses, so much I will confess:
But ne'er shall you, back to the land you left,
To dame or damsel return to boast yourself
That e'er you spoiled me to the tune of two pence,
Or made your profit of me or other men."
This done, to Roland he cries aloud for help.

AOI

147

Oliver feels he's wounded mortally;
His thirst for vengeance can never glutted be.
Amid the press he strikes right valiantly;
He breaks asunder the spear-shaft and the shield,
Splits chines and saddles and lops off hands and feet.
Whoso had seen him hew Paynims piece from piece,
Throw one on other their bodies down in heaps,
Might well remember that flower of knightly deeds!
And Carlon's war-cry he fails not to repeat,
But still "Mountjoy!" goes shouting loud and clear.
He calls to Roland his comrade and his peer:
"Sir, my companion, draw nigh and stand with me;
We must this day be parted to our grief."

                                                    AOI

148

Oliver's face, when Roland on him looks,
Is grey and ghastly, discoloured, wan with wounds,
His bright blood sprays his body head to foot;
Down to the ground it runs from him in pools.
"God!" says the Count, "I know not what to do!
Fair sir, companion, woe worth your mighty mood! –
Ne'er shall be seen a man to equal you.
Alas, fair France! what valiant men and true
Must thou bewail this day, cast down and doomed!
Bitter the loss the Emperor has to rue!"
So much he says, and in the saddle swoons.

                                                    AOI

149

See Roland now swooning in saddle laid,
And Oliver that unto death is maimed;
He's bled so much that his eyes are all glazed,
Or far or near he can see nothing straight,
Nor recognise a single living shape;
So when he comes to where his comrade waits,
On the gold helm he smites at him amain,
Down to the nasal he splits the jewelled plates,
Only his head is not touched by the blade.
Then Roland, stricken, lifts his eyes to his face,
Asking him low and mildly as he may:
"Sir, my companion, did you mean it that way?
Look, I am Roland, that loved you all my days;
You never sent me challenge or battle-gage."
Quoth Oliver: "I cannot see you plain;
I know your voice; may God see you and save.
And I have struck you; pardon it me, I pray."
Roland replies: "I have taken no scathe;
I pardon you, myself and in God's name."
Then each to other bows courteous in his place.
With such great love thus is their parting made.

150

Oliver feels the coming pangs of death;
Both of his eyes are turning in his head,
Now he is blind wholly, and wholly deaf.
He lights from horse and to his knees he gets

L. 2002 *challenge or battle-gage* – Roland wonders whether Oliver is still angry with him, but cannot believe that he would bear arms against him without having sent him a formal challenge, accompanied by the usual token of defiance (see below, Note to LL. 3875 sqq).

And makes confession aloud, and beats his breast,
Then clasps his hands and lifts them up to Heav'n;
In Paradise he prays God give him rest,
And France the Fair and Carlon prays Him bless,
And his companion Roland above all men.
His heart-strings crack, he stoops his knightly helm,
And sinks to earth, and lies there all his length.
Dead is the Count, his days have reached their end.
The valiant Roland weeps for him and laments,
No man on earth felt ever such distress.

151

When Roland sees his friend and comrade die,
And on the ground face down beholds him lie,
With tender words he bids him thus goodbye:
"Sir, my companion, woe worth your valiant might!
Long years and days have we lived side by side,
Ne'er didst thou wrong me nor suffer wrong of mine.
Now thou art dead I grieve to be alive."
Having thus said, the Marquis swoons outright
On his steed's back, that Veillantif is hight;
He's kept from falling by the gold stirrups bright;
Go as he may, they hold him still upright.

152

Or ever Roland comes to himself again
And has recovered and rallied from his faint,
Fearful disaster his fortunes have sustained;
All of the French are lost to him and slain;
Sole, the Archbishop and Walter Hum remain.

L. 2031 *marquis* – the title means "lord of the marches" (see note on L. 839).
Roland was Lord of the Marches of Brittany.

Walter has come down from the heights again;
Well has he striven against the men of Spain,
His men are dead, mown down by Paynim blades;
Will he or nill he, he flees towards the vale,
And upon Roland he cries aloud for aid:
"Where art thou, where, great county, warrior brave?
While thou wast there I never was dismayed.
Walter am I, who Maëlgut o'ercame,
Nephew am I to Droön white with age;
Thou for my valour wast wont to love me aye!
My lance is shattered, my shield is split in twain,
Battered and broken is my hauberk of mail,
A spear has pierced me [through the midst of my reins;]
Death is upon me, yet dear I made them pay."
Lo! at that word Roland hears him and wakes;
He spurs his horse and comes to him in haste.

AOI

153

Roland is filled with grief and anger sore;
In the thick press he now renews his war.
Of those of Spain he's overthrown a score,
And Walter six, the Archbishop five more.
The Paynims say: "These men are worst of all!
Let none escape alive; look to it, lords!
Who fears the onset, let shame be his reward!
Who lets these go, may he be put to scorn!"
Then once again the hue and cry breaks forth;
From every side pour in the Paynim hordes.

AOI

154

The County Roland is mighty of his mood,
Walter de Hum well-famed for knightlihood,
And the Archbishop a warrior tried and proved;
Betwixt their valours there's not a pin to choose.
In the thick press they smite the Moorish crew.
A thousand Paynims dismount to fight on foot,
And forty thousand horsemen they have, to boot,
Yet 'gainst these three, my troth! they fear to move.
They hurl against them their lances from aloof,
Javelins, jereeds, darts, shafts and spears they loose.
In the first shock brave Walter meets his doom.
Turpin of Rheims has his shield split in two,
His helm is broken, his head has ta'en a wound,
His hauberk's pierced, the mail-rings burst and strewn,
By four sharp spears his breast is stricken through,
Killed under him his horse rolls neck and croup;
Th'Archbishop's down, woe worth the bitter dule.

                                        AOI

155

Turpin of Rheims, finding himself o'erset,
With four sharp lance-heads stuck fast within his breast,
Quickly leaps up, brave lord, and stands erect.
He looks on Roland and runs to him and says
Only one word: "I am not beaten yet!
True man failed never while life in him was left."
He draws Almace, his steel-bright brand keen-edged;
A thousand strokes he strikes amid the press.
Soon Charles shall see he spared no foe he met,
For all about him he'll find four hundred men,
Some wounded, some clean through the body cleft,

L. 2082 *dule* - grief.

And some of them made shorter by the head.
So tells the Geste; so he that fought there tells:
The worthy Giles, whom God with marvels blessed,
In Laön minster thus-wise the charter penned;
Who knows not this knows nought of what befel.

156

The County Roland fights bravely as he may,
But his whole body in heat and sweat is bathed,
And all his head is racked with grievous pain
From that great blast which brake his temples' veins.
Fain would he know if Charles is bringing aid;
His Olifant he grasps, and blows full faint.
The Emperor halts, hearing the feeble strain:
"My lords," quoth he, "this tells a woeful tale;
Roland my nephew is lost to us this day,
That call proclaims his breath is nigh to fail.
Whoso would reach him must ride with desperate haste
Sound through the host! bid every trumpet play!"
Full sixty thousand so loud their clarions bray
The hills resound, the valleys ring again.
The Paynims hear, no lust to laugh have they:
"We'll soon have Charles to reckon with," they say.

AOI

157

The Paynims say: "The Emperor's turned about;
Of those of France hark how the trumpets sound!
If Carlon comes, we shall have rack and rout,
If Roland lives, once more he'll war us down,
We shall not keep one foot of Spanish ground."

L. 2096 *the worthy Giles* – St Giles, who had a hermitage in Provence, and became the hero of many legends.

Straightway four hundred helmed warriors rally round,
The finest fighters that in the field are found;
A fearful onslaught they'll make upon the Count;
Truly Lord Roland has got his work cut out.

158

Whenas Count Roland sees their assault begin,
Right fierce he makes him, and strong and menacing;
While life is in him he'll never quail or quit.
He sits his horse that is named Veillantif,
Into his flanks the golden spurs he pricks
And sets upon them where most the press is thick.
The Lord Archbishop, brave Turpin, rides with him.
Paynim to paynim cries: "Comrade, go to it!
Have we not heard the Frankish trumpets ring?
Charles is returning, the great, the mighty king!"

159

The County Roland ne'er loved a recreant,
Nor a false heart, nor yet a braggart jack,
Nor knight that was not a good man of his hands.
He cried to Turpin, the Churchman militant,
"Sir, you're on foot, I'm on my horse's back;
For love of you here will I make my stand,
And side by side we'll take both good and bad.
I'll not desert you for any mortal man.
Go we together these Paynims to attack;
The mightiest blows are those of Durendal."
Quoth the Archbishop: "'Twere shame our strokes to slack;
Carlon is coming, our vengeance shall not lack."

160

The Paynims say: "Why were we ever born?
Woe worth the while! our day of doom has dawned.
Now have we lost our peerage and our lords,
The mighty Carlon comes on with all his force,
Of those of France we hear the shrilling horns,
The cry "Mountjoy!" sounds fearfully abroad.
So grim of mood is Roland in his wrath
No man alive can put him to the sword.
Let fly at him, and then give up the war."
So they let fly; spears, lances they outpour,
Darts and jereeds and feathered shafts galore.
The shield of Roland is pierced and split and scored,
The mail-rings riven, and all his hauberk torn,
Yet in his body he is not touched at all,
Though under him, with thirty wounds and more,
His Veillantif is stricken dead and falls.
The Paynims flee, abandoning the war;
Count Roland's left amid the field, unhorsed.

AOI

161

In wrath and grief away the Paynims fly;
Backward to Spain with headlong haste they hie.
The County Roland cannot pursue their flight,
Veillantif's lost, he has no steed to ride;
Will he or nill he, he must on foot abide,
He's turned to aid Archbishop Turpin's plight,
And from his head the gilded helm untied,
Stripped off the hauberk of subtle rings and bright,
And all to pieces has cut the bliaut fine
Wherewith to bandage his wounds that gape so wide.
Then to his breast he clasps and lifts him light

And gently lays him upon the green hill-side,
With fair soft speech entreating on this wise:
"Ah, noble sir, pray give me leave awhile;
These friends of ours, we loved so well in life,
We must not leave them thus lying where they died.
I will go seek them, find, and identify,
And lay them here together in your sight."
"Go and return," the Bishop makes reply;
"Thanks be to God, this field is yours and mine."

162

Roland departs and through the field is gone;
Alone he searches the valleys and high rocks.
[And there he finds Ivor, and there Ivon],
Gerier and Gerin, the good companions,
[And Engelier whom Gascony begot];
And he has found Berenger and Oton,
And after finds Anseïs and Samson,
And finds Gerard the Old, of Roussillon.
He lifts them up, brave baron, one by one,
To the Archbishop he carries them anon,
And by his knees ranges them all along.
The Bishop weeps, he cannot stint thereof;
He lifts his hand and gives them benison,
And after saith: "Alack, brave champions!
May your souls rest with the all-glorious God
In Paradise, amid the rose-blossoms.
I too am dying and sorrow for my lot,
Who the great Emperor no more may look upon."

163

Roland once more unto the field repairs,
And has sought out his comrade Oliver.
Close to his breast he lifts him, and with care
As best he may to the Archbishop bears
And on his shield lays with the others there;
The Bishop signs and shrives them all with prayer.
With tears renewed their sorrow is declared,
And Roland saith: "Fair fellow Oliver,
You were own son unto Duke Renier
That held the marches of the Vale of Runers.
To shatter shield or break lance anywhere,
And from their seat proud men to overbear,
And cheer the brave with words of counsel fair,
And bring the cruel to ruin and despair,
No knight on earth was valiant as you were."

164

The County Roland, seeing his peers lie dead,
And Oliver, who was his dearest friend,
Begins to weep for ruth and tenderness;
Out of his cheeks the colour all has fled,
He cannot stand, he is so deep distressed,
He swoons to earth, he cannot help himself.
"Alas, for pity, sweet lord!" the Bishop saith.

165

When the Archbishop saw Roland faint and fallen,
So sad was he, he never had been more so;
He reaches out; he's taken Roland's horn up.
In Ronceval there runs a stream of water;

Fain would he go there and fetch a little for him.
With feeble steps he turns him thither, falt'ring;
He is so weak, that he cannot go forward,
For loss of blood he has no strength to call on.
Ere one might cover but a rood's length in walking
His heart has failed him, he has fallen face-foremost;
The pangs of death have seized him with great torment.

166

The County Roland has rallied from his faint,
Gets to his feet, though he's in grievous pain,
And looks about him over hill, over vale.
Beyond his comrades, upon the grass-green plain,
There he beholds the noble baron laid,
The great Archbishop, vice-gerent of God's name.
He beats his breast with eyes devoutly raised,
With folded hands lifted to Heaven he prays
That God will give him in Paradise a place.
Turpin is dead that fought for Charlemayn;
In mighty battles, and in preaching right brave,
Still against Paynims a champion of the Faith;
Blest mote he be, the Lord God give him grace!

AOI

167

The County Roland sees the Archbishop lie;
He sees his bowels gush forth out of his side
And on his brow the brain laid bare to sight.
Midst of his breast where the key-bones divide,
Crosswise he lays his comely hands and white,
And thus laments him as native use requires:
"Ah, debonair, thou good and noble knight!
Now I commend thee to the great Lord of might,

137

Servant more willing than thee He shall not find.
Since the Apostles no prophet was thy like,
For to maintain the Faith, and win mankind.
May thy soul meet no hindrance in her flight!
May Heaven's gate to her stand open wide!"

168

Now Roland feels that he is at death's door;
Out of his ears the brain is running forth.
Now for his peers he prays God call them all,
And for himself St Gabriel's aid implores;
Then in each hand he takes, lest shame befal,
His Olifant and Durendal his sword.
Far as a quarrel flies from a cross-bow drawn,
Toward land of Spain he goes, to a wide lawn,
And climbs a mound where grows a fair tree tall,
And marble stones beneath it stand by four.
Face downward there on the green grass he falls,
And swoons away, for he is at death's door.

169

High are the hills and very high the trees are;
Four stones there are set there, of marble gleaming.
The County Roland lies senseless on the greensward.
A Saracen is there, watching him keenly;
He has feigned death, and lies among his people,
And has smeared blood upon his breast and features.
Now he gets up and runs towards him fleetly;
Strong was he, comely and of valour exceeding.
Now in his rage and in his overweening
He falls on Roland, his arms and body seizing;

L. 2268 *marble stones* – probably posts such as were used to mark a frontier.

He saith one word: "Now Carlon's nephew's beaten.
I'll take his sword, to Araby I'll reive it."
But as he draws it Roland comes to, and feels him.

170

Roland has felt his good sword being stol'n;
Opens his eyes and speaks this word alone:
"Thou'rt none of ours, in so far as I know."
He takes his horn, of which he kept fast hold,
And smites the helm, which was all gemmed with gold;
He breaks the steel and the scalp and the bone,
And from his head batters his eyes out both,
And dead on ground he lays the villain low;
Then saith: "False Paynim, and how wast thou so bold,
Foully or fairly, to seize upon me so?
A fool he'll think thee who hears this story told.
Lo, now! the mouth of my Olifant's broke;
Fallen is all the crystal and the gold."

171

Now Roland feels his sight grow dim and weak;
With his last strength he struggles to his feet;
All the red blood has faded from his cheeks.
A grey stone stands before him at his knee:
Ten strokes thereon he strikes, with rage and grief;
It grides, but yet nor breaks nor chips the steel.
"Ah!" cries the Count, "St Mary succour me!
Alack the day, Durendal, good and keen!
Now I am dying, I cannot fend for thee.
How many battles I've won with you in field!
With you I've conquered so many goodly fiefs

L. 2282 *reive* – steal away.

That Carlon holds, the lord with the white beard!
Let none e'er wield you that from the foe would flee –
You that were wielded so long by a good liege!
The like of you blest France shall never see."

172

Count Roland smites the sardin stone amain.
The steel grides loud, but neither breaks nor bates.
Now when he sees that it will nowise break
Thus to himself he maketh his complaint:
"Ah, Durendal! so bright, so brave, so gay!
How dost thou glitter and shine in the sun's rays!
When Charles was keeping the vales of Moriane,
God by an angel sent to him and ordained
He should bestow thee on some count-capitayne.
On me he girt thee, the noble Charlemayn.
With this I won him Anjou and all Bretayn,
With this I won him Poitou, and conquered Maine;
With this I won him Normandy's fair terrain,
And with it won Provence and Acquitaine,
And Lombardy and all the land Romayne,
Bavaria too, and the whole Flemish state,
And Burgundy and all Apulia gained;
Constantinople in the King's hand I laid;
In Saxony he speaks and is obeyed;
With this I won Scotland, [Ireland and Wales,]
And England, where he set up his domain;
What lands and countries I've conquered by its aid,
For Charles to keep whose beard is white as may!
Now am I grieved and troubled for my blade;

L. 2331 – the text is corrupt; but either Ireland or Wales is certainly
intended, and possibly both.

Should Paynims get it, 'twere worse than all death's pains.
Dear God forbid it should put France to shame!"

173

Count Roland smites upon the marble stone;
I cannot tell you how he hewed it and smote;
Yet the blade breaks not nor splinters, though it groans;
Upward to heaven it rebounds from the blow.
When the Count sees it never will be broke,
Then to himself right softly he makes moan:
"Ah, Durendal, fair, hallowed, and devote,
What store of relics lie in thy hilt of gold!
St Peter's tooth, St Basil's blood, it holds,
Hair of my lord St Denis, there enclosed,
Likewise a piece of Blessed Mary's robe;
To Paynim hands 'twere sin to let you go;
You should be served by Christian men alone,
Ne'er may you fall to any coward soul!
Many wide lands I conquered by your strokes
For Charles to keep whose beard is white as snow,
Whereby right rich and mighty is his throne."

174

Now Roland feels death press upon him hard;
It's creeping down from his head to his heart.
Under a pine-tree he hastens him apart,
There stretches him face down on the green grass,
And lays beneath him his sword and Olifant.
He's turned his head to where the Paynims are,
And this he doth for the French and for Charles,
Since fain is he that they should say, brave heart,
That he has died a conquerer at the last.

He beats his breast full many a time and fast,
Gives, with his glove, his sins into God's charge.

AOI

175

Now Roland feels his time is at an end;
On the steep hill-side, toward Spain he's turned his head,
And with one hand he beats upon his breast;
Saith: "*Mea culpa*; Thy mercy, Lord, I beg
For all the sins, both the great and the less,
That e'er I did since first I drew my breath
Unto this day when I'm struck down by death."
His right-hand glove he unto God extends;
Angels from Heaven now to his side descend.

AOI

176

The County Roland lay down beneath a pine;
To land of Spain he's turned him as he lies,
And many things begins to call to mind:
All the broad lands he conquered in his time,
And fairest France, and the men of his line,
And Charles his lord, who bred him from a child;
He cannot help but weep for them and sigh.
Yet of himself he is mindful betimes;
He beats his breast and on God's mercy cries:
"Father most true, in whom there is no lie,
Who didst from death St Lazarus make to rise,
And bring out Daniel safe from the lions' might,
Save Thou my soul from danger and despite
Of all the sins I did in all my life."
His right-hand glove he's tendered unto Christ,

And from his hand Gabriel accepts the sign.
Straightway his head upon his arm declines;
With folded hands he makes an end and dies.
God sent to him His Angel Cherubine,
And great St Michael of Peril-by-the-Tide;
St Gabriel too was with them at his side;
The County's soul they bear to Paradise.

177

Roland is dead, in Heaven God hath his soul.
The Emperor Charles rides in to Roncevaux.
No way there is therein, nor any road,
No path, no yard, no foot of naked mould
But there some French or Paynim corpse lies strown.
Charles cries: "Where are you, fair nephew? Out, harò!
Where's the Archbishop? is Oliver laid low?
Where are Gerin, Gerier his playfellow,
And Berenger, and the good Count Othone?
Ivor and Ives, so well I loved them both?
Where's Engelier, the Gascon great of note?
Samson the Duke, and Anseïs the Bold?
And where is Gerard of Roussillon the Old?
Where the Twelve Peers I left to guard the host?"
What use to cry? all's still as any stone.
"God!" says the King, "how bitter my reproach,
That I was absent when they struck the first blow!"
He plucks his beard right angerly and wroth;
Barons and knights all weep and make their moan,

LL. 2390-91 *the sign* – The glove is offered and accepted in token of Roland's
surrender to God of the life which he holds as a fief from Him. Compare
Marsilion's surrender to Baligant of the fief of Spain (LL. 2830-2838).
L. 2393 *Cherubine* – "Cherubin" seems to be used by the poet as the name
of an individual angel.

Full twenty thousand swoon to the ground for woe;
Naimon the Duke is grieved with all his soul.

178

There is no baron nor knight in all the train
That does not weep most piteously for pain;
Brothers and sons and nephews they bewail
For their liege-lords and friends they make complaint;
Many of them fall to the ground and faint.
Great wisdom then Naimon the Duke displays,
For to the Emperor he is the first to say:
"Look there ahead, perchance two leagues away,
Those clouds of dust, the highway in a haze –
See how great hordes of Paynims flee apace!
Ride, my lord, ride! avenge this dolorous fray!"
"Alas!" quoth Charles, "what an advance they've gained!
Truly you counsel what right and honour claim;
Fair France's flower they've reft from me this day."
He summons Othon and Geboïn to aid,
Tibbald of Rheims and County Milon brave:
"Guard you the field, guard all the hills and vales;
As the dead lie, so let them lie, I say;
Let no lion touch them nor any beast of prey,
Nor any squire touch them, nor any knave,
I charge you, none – no hand on them be laid,
Till to this field, please God, we come again."
And they reply with love and reverence great:
"Most dearest lord, just Emperor, we obey."
Of their meinie a thousand knights they name.

AOI

L. 2432 *Othon* – not, of course, the Othon who was one of the Twelve Peers killed in the battle, but Othon the Marquis, one of Charlemayn's barons, mentioned again in LL. 2971, 3057.

179

The Emperor bids the trumpets sound to war;
With his whole army the valiant king sets forth;
Hard on the trail they chase, with one accord,
The men of Spain whose backs are turned far off.
When the King sees the dusk begin to fall,
In a green meadow he lights down on the sward,
Kneels on the ground and prays to God Our Lord
For love of him to hold back the sun's course,
Prolong the day and bid the dark withdraw.
Straightway an angel with whom he wont to talk
Comes, with this summons, in answer to his call:
"Ride, Carlon, ride; the light shall not come short!
The flower of France is fallen; God knows all;
Thou shalt have vengeance upon the heathen horde."
When this he hears, the Emperor gets to horse.

AOI

180

For Charlemayn God wrought a wondrous token:
The sun stood still in the mid-heaven holden.
The Paynims flee, the French pursue them closely.
They overtake them in Vale of Tenebrosa.
Toward Saragossa they drive and beat them broken,
With mighty strokes they slay them in their going,
Cut their retreat off by the highways and roadways.
The River Ebro confronts them swiftly-flowing
And very deep and most fearfully swollen;
There is no barge, neither lighter nor dromond.
In desperation their Termagant invoking,
The Paynims plunge, but their gods take no notice.
Those that are armed in heavy helm and hauberk
Sink to the bottom in numbers past all noting.

Others drift downstream upon the current floating;
Happiest is he who promptly gets his throatful,
They are all drowned in a welter most woeful:
The French cry: "Luckless the day you looked on Roland!"

AOI

181

When Charles sees all the Paynims dead past doubt,
Some of them slain and the greater part drowned,
On whose rich spoils his chivalry can count,
The noble King from his charger dismounts
And gives God thanks, kneeling upon the ground.
When he arises he finds the sun gone down.
The Emperor says: "'Tis time to camp, I trow;
To Ronceval too late to turn back now,
Because our horses are jaded and tired out;
Unloose the saddles, take the bits from their mouths,
Let them go graze these meadows all around."
The French reply: "Sire, your advice is sound."

AOI

182

The Emperor now has his encampment set;
In open country afoot are all the French;
They've freed their horses from saddle and from belt,
The golden bridles they've loosed from off their heads
And let them run where grass grows thick and fresh:
That is as much as they can do for them.
Whoso is weary has made the earth his bed;
And for that night they post no sentinels.

183

In a green meadow the Emperor Charles is laid,
Beside his head his mighty spear is placed,
He'll not, this night, put off his war-array;
He's clad in hauberk of shining saffron mail,
Hath on his head his gold-gemmed helmet laced,
And, girt about him, Joyeuse, his peerless blade,
That changes colour full thirty times a day.
You know the lance – for oft we've heard the tale –
Which pierced Our Lord when He on cross was slain:
Carlon possesses the lancehead, God be praised!
In the gold pummel he's had it shrined and cased,
And for to honour such favour and such grace
This sword of his is called Joyeuse by name.
Barons of France can scarce forget that same,
For then 'Mountjoy', their battle-cry, was made;
Wherefore no nation can stand before their face.

184

The night is clear and the moon shining bright;
Charles lies awake and weeps for Roland's plight,
For Oliver he weeps with all his might,
Weeps his Twelve Peers, his French folk left behind
In Roncevaux, slain bloodily in fight.
He cannot help but mourn for them and sigh,
And pray God bring their souls to Paradise.
The King is weary, for grief weighs on his eyes;
He can no more, he sleeps after a while,
And all the French sleep in the field likewise.
There's not a horse has strength to stand upright;

L. 2510 *Mountjoy* – this derivation, which has no foundation in fact, is
probably due to the poet's own ingenuity. See note on L. 1181.

If they want grass they crop it as they lie.
He that has suffered learns many things in life.

185

Carlon is sleeping as one worn out with grief.
St Gabriel comes, sent from his heavenly seat
To guard the Emperor, by God's express decree.
Watch at his head all night the Angel keeps,
And shows to him, in likeness of a dream,
A battle new, which he will have to meet;
By grievous portents the meaning is revealed.
Looking to heaven stands Carlon, so it seems;
There he beholds great gales and tempests beat,
Levin and hail and fearful storms and sleet,
And fire and flame kindled, falling in sheets
All of a sudden upon his host a-field;
Burning the lances of ash and apple-beam,
E'en the gold bosses burning upon the shields,
Riving in sunder the shafts of the sharp spears,
Splitting the hauberks and the helmets of steel;
In great distress he sees his chivalry.
Then to devour them come bears, and leopards keen,
Worms, wyverns, dragons, and devils from the deep,
And thirty thousand griffins along with these,
That on the French come pouncing all and each.
The French cry, "Help! O Charlemayn, make speed!"
Anguish of heart and pity the King feels;
Fain would he hasten, but fresh woes intervene.
A mighty lion out of a forest leaps,

LL. 2530–2553 *a battle new*, etc. – This passage, which bears no detailed
relation to the events which it foreshadows, and may be imitated from a
classical source, refers to the battle with the oriental Paynims (the strange
beasts) and the single combat of Charlemayn with Baligant (the lion).
L. 2543 *worms* – a general term for any kind of reptilian monsters.

Haughty and fierce and terrible to see;
His royal body it would attack and seize;
They clasp each other and grapple, man to beast,
Nor can he tell who's top and who's beneath.
The Emperor slumbers, he wakes not from his sleep.

186

After this vision the Emperor dreamed again:
That on a dais he stood, in France, at Aix,
Leading a bear bound with a double chain;
And from Ardennes thirty more bears there came,
Each one of which spoke in a human way.
"Sire, give him back to us," they seemed to say;
"For in your hand he ought not to remain;
He is our kinsman and we must give him aid."
Out of the palace he sees a greyhound race,
Sees it attack the biggest bear apace;
On the green grass beyond them all, straightway
The King beholds a wondrous fierce affray,
But cannot tell which one will win the day.
These things God's Angel to the good King displays.
Carlon sleeps on till the bright morning breaks.

187

Marsile has fled to Saragossa town.
Beneath an olive in the shade he dismounts,
Resigns his sword, his helm, his byrny brown,

LL. 2555-2567 *the Emperor dreamed again* – this vision foretells the trial of
Ganelon (the bear), the intervention of his kinsmen (the other bears), and
the single combat between Thierry (the greyhound) and Pinabel (the biggest
bear).
L. 2572 *brown* – burnished.

On the green grass lies miserably down;
His right hand's gone and he must do without;
For pain and loss of blood he falls in swound.
Before him comes Queen Bramimond his spouse,
Wails and laments and utters dismal sounds.
By twenty thousand his followers stand around;
They curse fair France and Carlon they denounce.
Apollyon's grotto they make for in a rout,
With ugly insults they threaten him and shout:
"Aha! vile god, why must thou shame us now?
Why let disaster befal this king of ours?
To faithful servants a generous lord art thou!"
They snatch away his sceptre and his crown,
By his hands hang him upon a column bound,
And with thick cudgels belabour him and pound;
Then with their feet trample him on the ground.
Termagant gets his carbuncle torn out;
Into a ditch they boot away Mahound
For pigs and dogs to mangle and befoul.

188

The King Marsile recovers him from fainting,
He bids them bear him into his vaulted chamber
That in bright colours is all inscribed and painted.
And there his wife, Queen Bramimond, bewails him:
She tears her hair and cries: "Ah! wretched lady!"
And at each word loudly laments her, saying:
"Ah, Saragossa! desolate thou remainest
For this great king that was thy lord and safeguard!

LL. 2587–8 I have ventured to transpose these two lines, so as to provide a
more plausible function for the "column". I think the picture is that of a
criminal tied by the hands to a column and flogged, as in many illustrations
of the scourging of Christ.

Truly, our gods have acted very basely
Who in the battle this day forsook and failed him.
And the Emir will show himself a craven
Not to give battle unto this race courageous
Who are so reckless, they hold their lives as playthings.
Yea, and this Emperor of theirs, this ancient greybeard,
Is so o'erweening and carries him so bravely,
He'll never flee if war is in the waging.
Alas for pity that there is none to slay him!"

189

The Emperor Charles by force of arms and skill
Full seven years long in Spain has sojourned still,
Made many a city and many a castle his.
Marsile has done his utmost to resist:
In the first year letters went out from him
To Baligant in Babylon – that is
To the Emir: an ancient old man this;
Homer and Virgil alike he has outlived:
To Saragossa let him bring succour swift;
If not, Marsile his paynim gods will quit.
Leave all the idols he worships (saith the writ),
To the blest faith of Christendom submit,
And make his peace with Charlemayn the King.
There's been delay; far off the Emir lives.
From forty realms he's called his people in;
His mighty dromonds he has at length equipped,
Carracks and barges, galleys and fighting ships;
In Alexandria, where the wide harbour dips
Down to the sea, his whole fleet ready sits.
In May, the day when summer first begins,
With all his armies he looses from the slips.

190

Huge are the forces of this detested race.
The Paynims voyage, steering with oars and sail.
On the tall prows and on the masts they raise
Unnumbered lanterns and carbuncles ablaze;
High overhead they throw out such a flame,
The sea by night is beautiful and gay;
And when they draw unto the land of Spain
The whole coast shines and glitters in the rays.
Marsile hears news that they are on the way.

AOI

191

The Paynim hosts press on with all their might;
They leave the sea, the freshets now they find;
They leave Marbrise, they leave Marbrose behind,
And up the Ebro the whole fleet turns and glides.
With carbuncles and countless lanterns bright
From dusk to dawn they have abundant light,
And the next day in Saragossa lie.

AOI

192

Clear is the day, the sun shines fair to see.
Forth of the ship the great Emir proceeds;
At his right hand there goes Espanelis,

L. 2633 *carbuncles* – the carbuncle was credited with much magical power,
and was confidently believed to shine by its own light. In folk-lore and
fairy-tale we frequently find enchanted palaces "lit by a single carbuncle,"
as for instance the under-water palace of Fata Morgana in Boiardo's *Orlando
Innamorato* (whose hero, incidentally, is Count Roland himself, much
changed and romanticised), or the underground palace of the King of
Elfland in the English tale of Childe Rowland (the knight who "to the
Dark Tower came"; no relation of Charlemagne's Roland, so far as I know).

And sev'nteen kings follow him at the heel;
I cannot reckon what dukes and counts there be.
In a fair meadow, beneath a laurel-tree,
A snow-white cloth is spread on the green lea;
On it they place a throne of ivory.
There Baligant the Paynim takes his seat,
And his whole train stand round him on their feet.
First of them all their lord and master speaks:
"Now lithe and listen, my valiant knights and free!
The Emperor Charles, that holds the Franks in fee,
Shall not eat bread except I give him leave.
He's warred against me in Spain right grievously;
Now to fair France go I, his might to meet,
And while I live from war I will not cease
Till he be dead or, living, yield to me."
With his right glove he smites upon his knee.

193

He speaks; and swears an oath to this effect:
That he'll not fail, for all the gold 'neath heav'n,
To go to Aix, where Carlon's courts are held.
His men, applauding, advise just what he says.
Now has he summoned two knights from out the rest –
Clarifant's one, the other Clarïen:
"You are the sons of that King Maltraïen
Who oft as envoy served me with glad consent.
To Saragossa I bid you journey hence,
And, as from me, this to Marsilion tell:
That to his aid I've come, against the French;
Great war I'll wage where'er I light on them.
Give him this folded glove with golden hems;
On his right hand make sure you see it set.

L. 2657 *lithe* – hearken.

Give him this wand of purest gold as well;
Bid him come seek me and here his fealty pledge.
I go to France to fight Charles to the death.
If at my feet he bow not down his neck,
If he renounce not the faith of Christian men,
Then will I take the crown from off his head."
The Paynims say: "Sir, that is right well said."

194

Quoth Baligant: "To horse, my lords! Ride on!
Take one the glove, the other take the wand."
"Dear sir, we will", the pair make answer prompt.
To Saragossa they ride and come anon.
They pass ten gates, four bridges pass across,
And thread the streets wherein the burghers lodge.
And when at last they reach the city's top,
Before the palace they hear loud cries and long.
Here many paynims are gathered in a throng
Wailing and howling in accents woebegone
For Termagant and for Mahound, their gods,
And for Apollyon, who unto them are lost.
Each cries: "Woe's me! what now will be our lot?
Fearful disaster is fall'n on us headlong!
Lo! we have lost our King Marsilion,
Roland the Count has cut his right hand off;
And Jurfaret the Fair, he too is gone.
Today all Spain will lie beneath their rod!"
Down light the envoys the terrace steps upon.

195

Beneath an olive they leave their horses waiting;
Two Saracens to hold the reins have hastened.
Then, each one holding his fellow by the raiment,
The envoys enter, the lofty palace scaling.
When they are come into the vaulted chamber
Friendly they proffer ill-omened salutation:
"Now may Mahound, that hath us in his safeguard,
And Lord Apollyon, and Termagant, with favour
Protect the King, and to the Queen be gracious!"
Quoth Bramimond: "Why, there's a foolish saying!
These gods of ours are miserable traitors.
They have worked wonders at Roncevaux, the caitiffs!
They let our knights be slaughtered there unaided.
As for my lord, they've utterly betrayed him;
His right hand's gone, there's not a doit remaining;
'Twas smitten off by Roland, the Count makeless.
Now Charlemayn has all Spain for the taking.
And what of me, forlorn and wretched lady?
Woe worth the day! Why is there none to slay me?"
                                                    AOI

196

Quoth Clarien: "Lady, bridle your tongue awhile.
From Baligant the Paynim we've arrived.
Help for Marsile he says he will provide;
His glove and wand he sends you for a sign.
On Ebro now four thousand vessels ride,
Barges and boats and racing galleys light
And dromonds, more than I can count, beside.
Our great Emir is rich, unmatched for might;
To France he'll go, Charlemayn there to find,

L. 2720 *makeless* – peerless.

155

And make him yield, or slay him else outright."
Quoth Bramimond: "As far as France? fie, fie!
We've Franks a-plenty nearer by many a mile.
These sev'n years past they've been here all the time.
The Emperor Charles is stout and full of fight.
Flee from the field? not he; he'd rather die.
The best king living he rates but as a child;
Charles has no fear of any man alive."

197

"Have done, have done," then said the King Marsile;
And to the envoys: "To me, sirs, pray you speak.
I'm at death's door, as you may plainly see.
No son, no daughter, no heir have I to leave;
One son I had and he was killed yestre'en.
Ask the Emir to come and visit me;
On land of Spain a right good claim has he;
If he will have it, to him I yield it free;
Let him defend it against these Frankish thieves.
With Charlemayn I'll tell him how to deal,
And in a month he'll beat him to his knees.
Of Saragossa go, carry him the keys,
To have and hold, if he will mark my rede."
"Sir," they reply, "your words are wise indeed."

AOI

198

Then said Marsile: "The Emperor of the Franks
Has slain my vassals and wasted all my lands,
My cities too he has destroyed and sacked.
He lay last night upon the Ebro's bank;
Not sev'n leagues off, I reckon, is his camp.
Bid the Emir his utmost power dispatch;

By you I charge him to march to the attack."
The city's keys he puts into their hands.
Then the two envoys obsequious bowed their backs,
Bade him farewell, and took the homeward track.

199

The messengers upon their horses get.
Forth of the city fast as they may they press;
To the Emir they come in much distress;
Of Saragossa the keys to him present.
Quoth Baligant: "What news have you to tell?
Where is the King, Marsile, for whom I sent?"
Clarïen answers: "He is wounded to death.
Yesterday Charles towards the passes went;
To make return to France was his intent;
And in his rear a noble guard he set:
The County Roland, his nephew, there he left,
And Oliver, and all the Peers, all twelve.
With them in arms were twenty thousand French.
The valiant King, Marsile, upon them fell,
And in the field he and Count Roland met;
There such a blow by Durendal was dealt,
Marsile's right hand was from his body cleft.
Also his son, whom well he loved, is dead,
And slain are all the barons whom he led.
Endure he could not, but from the battle fled.
Carlon pursued him for many a long stretch.
Now the King prays that you will bring him help,
And unto you bequeaths the Spanish realm."
Now Baligant must needs bethink himself;
With rage and grief he's almost off his head.

                                        AOI

200

"My Lord Emir," quoth Clariën again,
"In Roncevaux was battle yesterday.
Roland is dead, Count Oliver is slain,
And the Twelve Peers beloved of Charlemayn;
By twenty thousand the French lie dead on plain.
Clean from his body Marsile's right hand is razed;
Right furiously the Emperor pressed the chase.
There's not a knight in all this land remains
But has been killed, or drowned in Ebro's wave.
Upon the bank the French their camp have made:
If you strike now, they lie so near this place
That they will find it full hard to get away."
Baligant hears: right haughty is his face,
And in his heart joyous he is and gay;
Up from his throne he leaps and stands full straight.
He cries aloud: "Come, barons, no delay!
Out of the ships! to horse! and ride in haste!
Unless by flight old Charlemayn escape,
The King Marsile shall be avenged this day,
And head for hand I'll give him in exchange."

201

Out of the ships the Arab Paynims move;
Straightway they've mounted their horses and their mules,
And forth they rode; what better could they do?
Then the Emir, who stirred this warlike brew,
Summoned Gemalfin, a minion of his crew,
Saying: "I give thee command of all my troops."
Then mounts his steed whose coat is brown of hue,
And as his escort he takes with him four dukes.
To Saragossa his journey he pursued,

And on a terrace lit down, of marble hewn;
To hold his stirrup four counts together stoop.
He climbs the steps under the palace roof;
There Bramimonda comes running him unto.
She cries to him: "Woe's me! the dreadful news!
My lord is dying a shameful death undue!"
She falls before him, he lifts her up anew;
Into the chamber they come, in doleful mood.

                                          AOI

202

When King Marsile sees the Emir come in,
At once he summons two Spanish Sarrasins:
"Lend me your arms, raise me that I may sit."
In his left hand one of his gloves he grips.
Then saith Marsile: "My Lord Emir and King,
See! this whole country [into your hand I give,]
And Saragossa and all its fiefs herewith.
Myself I've lost, my people, and my kin."
And he replies: "I'm deeply grieved for this.
I must not stay a long time parleying;
Charles will get moving, right well I know he will,
Nevertheless, I take your glove and gift."
Weeping he turns, such grief his bosom fills,
Descends the steps, and so the palace quits.
He gets to horse and joins his men forthwith;
He overtakes them all, he spurs so swift,
And rides ahead, shouting aloud by fits:
"Paynims, come on! e'en now they fly, methinks!"

                                          AOI

203

At crack of dawn, when daylight first draws on.
The Emperor Charles wakes from his sleep anon.
His watching angel, St Gabriel, sent from God,
Lifts up his hand and signs him with the cross.
The King ungirds, and takes his armour off,
And the whole host likewise their harness doff.
They get to horse and briskly ride along
Through the wide plains and up the roadways long.
They go to see the great and wondrous loss
At Roncevaux, there where the battle was.

AOI

204

To Roncevaux comes Carlon by and by.
He sees the dead, and tears come to his eyes.
He tells the French: "Slowly, sirs, pray you ride;
I would go first, alone, with none beside,
For I would fain my nephew's body find.
Yonder at Aix, one festal day, was I,
And all about me stood valiant men of mine,
Boasting of battles and of their fiercest fights.
Roland said something which now I call to mind:
That should he come in foreign lands to die,
Beyond them all, footmen or peers, he'd lie,
And have his face turned to the enemy;
Fighting he'd fall, and finish victor-like."
Before the rest a staff's cast or thereby
The Emperor goes and to a hill-top climbs.

205

As the King goes his nephew for to seek,
How many flowers he finds upon the lea
Red with the blood of all our chivalry!
He feels such pity he cannot choose but weep.
And now he reaches a place beneath two trees:
There, on three stones, Count Roland's strokes he sees,
And sees his nephew stretched on the grassy green.
It is no wonder if Carlon's woe is keen.
Straight he dismounts and runs there on his feet,
Between his hands he clasps the baron's cheeks,
And swoons upon him, he is so wrung with grief.

206

From out his swoon the Emperor's raised his head.
Naimon the Duke and County Acelon then,
Geoffrey d'Anjou, Henry his brother next,
Lift the King up against a pine-tree's stem.
He looks to earth and sees his nephew dead,
And very softly thus utters his lament:
"God show thee mercy, Count Roland, my dear friend!
So great a knight as thou was ne'er seen yet,
To undertake great wars and win them well.
Alas! my glory is sinking to its end!"
King Carlon swoons, he cannot help himself.

AOI

207

Carlon the King out of his swoon revives.
Four barons hold him between their hands upright.
He looks to earth and sees his nephew lie.
Fair is his body, but all his hue is white.

His upturned eyes are shadowy with night.
By faith and love Charles mourns him on this wise:
"Roland, my friend, God have thy soul on high
With the bright Hallows in flowers of Paradise!
Thy wretched lord sent thee to Spain to die!
Never shall day bring comfort to my eyes.
How fast must dwindle my joy now and my might!
None shall I have to keep my honour bright!
Methinks I've not one friend left under sky;
Kinsmen I have, but none that is thy like."
He tears his hair with both hands for despite.
By hundred thousand the French for sorrow sigh;
There's none of them but utters grievous cries.

                                                    AOI

208

"Roland, my friend to France I go again.
When I'm at Laon within my own domain
Many will come of alien realm and race
Asking: 'Where's he, the great Count Capitayne?'
And I must tell them that he lies dead in Spain.
All my life long in sorrow must I reign.
Nor any day cease grieving and complaint.

209

Roland, my friend, heart valiant, goodly youth,
When I'm at Aix, beneath my chapel roof,
Many will come, and they will ask for news.
Then must I tell them the strange and heavy truth:
'Dead is my nephew that all my realms subdued.'

L. 2910 *Laon* – this city was the royal seat of the later Carolingian monarchs, and as such known to the poet. He has here committed an anachronism in making it the seat of Charlemagne, who (as elsewhere he states quite correctly) had his chief residence at Aix-la-Chapelle.

Then will the Saxons rise up against my rule,
Hungarians, Bulgars and many a hostile brood,
From Rome, Palermo, Apulia to boot,
The Afric bands, the Califernian crew –
Then will my troubles and toils begin anew.
Where is the might that now shall lead my troops,
Since he is dead that always brought us through?
Alas, fair France, how desolate are you!
I am so wretched, would I had perished too."
He tears his beard that is so white of hue,
Tears with both hands his white hair by the roots;
And of the French an hundred thousand swoon.

210

"Roland, my friend, God bring thee to His rest,
And set thy soul in Paradise the blest!
He that slew thee hath ruined France as well.
So great my grief, I would that I were dead,
Grief for my household, thus slain in my defence!
Now grant me God that lay on Mary's breast
That ere my foot in Sizer pass be set,
Out of my body my spirit may be reft
And placed with theirs, along with them to dwell,
And under earth my flesh beside their flesh!"
He weeps for woe, his silver beard he rends.
Then saith Duke Naimon: "Charles is in great distress."

AOI

211

Geoffrey d'Anjou then spake, "Lord Emperor,
Pray you be calm and sorrow not so sore.
Have the field searched for all our men and lords
Whom those of Spain to death in battle brought,

And in one grave let them be buried all."
The King replies: "I will; go sound your horn!"

AOI

212

Geoffrey d'Anjou has made his trumpet sound.
By Carlon's orders the French straightway dismount.
When the dead bodies of all their friends are found,
In one great trench they lay them underground.
Bishops and abbots throughout the host abound,
Canons and monks, and priests with shaven crowns;
So in God's name they shrive and sign them now.
They kindle myrrh and incense in thick clouds
And cense them all with lavish hand all round;
Then with great honour they raise the burial-mound;
So there they leave them; what else were in their power?

AOI

213

Charles has had Roland prepared for burial-rites,
With Bishop Turpin and Oliver besides.
He's had their bodies opened before his eyes,
Had their hearts wrapped in silken tissue fine,
And placed within an urn of marble white.
The barons' bodies they then take up and wind
Straitly in shrouds made of the roebuck's hide,
Having first washed them with spices and with wine.
The King calls Tibbald and Gebuin to his side,
Othon the Marquis and Count Milon likewise:
"On three wains place them, and you must be their guides."
O'er each they throw a rich pall Galazine.

AOI

L. 2973 *Galazine* – of oriental material (from Galata, near Constantinople; or perhaps from Galatia or from Galazza, now Lajozzo, near Alexandretta).

214

All set for home stands now the Emperor Charles,
When lo! here come the Paynim's vanward guards!
Before them ride the envoys spurring fast
To bear the challenge of the Emir they're charged:
"Think not, proud king, thus scatheless to depart!
See, Baligant follows upon you hard.
With him he brings an Arab host full large;
Now shall we see if you are stout of heart!"
Over his beard King Carlon's fingers pass,
As he remembers his loss and bitter smart.
Proudly he looks on all the hosts of France;
Then loud and high he sends his voice out far:
"Barons of France, to horse now and to arms!"

AOI

215

The Emperor's first in arming for the field.
In his bright byrny he clothes him with all speed,
Laces his helm, girds on his sword of steel,
Joyeuse, whose blade outshines the sun's own sheen,
Hangs on his neck his stout Viterbo shield,
And takes his spear, tossing it by the beam.
Then he bestrides Tencendur his good steed –
At Marsonne ford erewhile he won the beast,
Hurling Malpallin of Narbonne from his seat;
He spurs him hard, shaking the bridle free,
And goes a-gallop for all his men to see,
Calling on God and him that bare the Keys.

AOI

216

Throughout the field the French dismount straightway,
An hundred thousand and more put on their mail.
For their equipment they've all that heart could crave,
Swift running steeds and weapons well arrayed.
They mount and show their manage and their pace;
When the time comes they mean to fight amain.
Down to their helms the gonfalons float gay.
When Carlon sees how splendidly they shape,
Thus to Duke Naimon, Antelme of Mayence brave,
And Joz'rain of Provence he says his say:
"In such as these a man may well have faith;
With these about one to doubt would be insane.
We'll make these Arabs repent that e'er they came;
For Roland's death I think they'll dearly pay."
Duke Naimon answers: "God grant it so, I pray!"

AOI

217

Carlon has called Rabel and Guinemant,
Then saith the King: "You, sirs, I now command
In Roland's stead and Oliver's to stand:
Take one the sword and one the Olifant,
And ride ahead as leaders of the van,
With fifteen thousand good Frenchmen at your backs,
Young bachelors all, the bravest in the land.
Then, a like number shall form a second band
By Geboïn led and with him Guinemant."
Naimon the Duke and the Count Jozeran
Marshal the columns according to this plan.
Great work there'll be when these fight hand to hand.

AOI

218

The first two columns are made up of the French.
And the third column, which they establish next,
Is formed entirely of stout Bavarian men:
Knights twenty thousand make up its complement,
Their line of battle will never break nor bend;
Charles holds them dear as any under heav'n,
Save his own Frenchmen who won him such wide realms.
Ogier the Dane, good Count, is at their head;
Great troops are they, and he a warrior dread.

AOI

219

Three columns now has Charles the Emperor;
Next, the Duke Naimon establishes a fourth,
This is made up of very valiant lords,
Germans are they, and all in Almayn born;
Full twenty thousand, or so the rest report,
With arms and horses very well furnished forth;
They'll never flinch, though they should perish all.
Hermann, the Duke of Trace, leads them to war;
He'd rather die than quail or suffer scorn.

AOI

220

Naimon the Duke and the Count Jozeran
Choose for the fifth men from the Norman lands.
At twenty thousand they're reckoned by the Franks.
Well horsed are they, well harnessed, every man;
They'd rather die than they would turn their backs,
And under heaven you scarce could find their match.
Richard the Old is leader of their ranks,
He'll strike good blows with his sharp lance in hand.

AOI

221

In the sixth column are men of Brittany;
Full thirty thousand they count their chivalry.
They ride along, a gallant sight to see,
With painted spears and pennons flying free.
Over this folk Eudon hath seigneury;
Othon the Marquis, Tibbald the Lord of Rheims,
Count Nevelon he calls, and thus he speaks:
"Pray lead my men; accept this boon of me."

AOI

222

The Emperor now has got six columns ready;
Naimon the Duke proceeds to make the seventh;
Lords of Auvergne and Poitou he's selected:
Knights forty thousand or thereabouts, 'tis reckoned.
Well are they armed and mounted on good destriers;
Down dale apart under a hill he sets them.
With his right hand Charles gives them all his blessing.
They're led by Godselm and Jozeran together.

AOI

223

And the eighth column Naimon disposes swiftly,
Composed of Flemings and the barons of Frisia.
Knights forty thousand or more maybe are with them;
Their battle-lines stand fast with ne'er a quiver.
"Better than these," quoth Charles, "I could not wish for.
Between them, Rembalt and Hamon of Galicia
Right valiantly shall govern this militia."

AOI

224

Count Jozeran and Naimon make no stop,
But the ninth column to valiant troops allot:
Men of Lorraine and of Burgundian stock;
Knights fifty thousand they estimate the throng.
Their helms are laced, their byrnies all are donned,
Short are their spears but made exceeding strong.
If the Arabians flinch not from battle-shock,
Once these get going they'll give them all they've got.
They're led by Thierry, the good duke of Argonne.

AOI

225

In the tenth column stand lords of France arrayed:
One hundred thousand of our best captains they;
Proudly they bear them, their bodies are full straight,
Their heads are grizzled, and all their beards are grey.
Hauberks they wear, byrnies of double mail,
Girded with swords well-forged in France or Spain;
They've splendid shields, with cognisances gay.
They mount their horses and clamour for the fray;
"Mountjoy!" they shout: with them is Charlemayn.
Geoffrey d'Anjou the oriflamme has raised;
It was St Peter's, and then was called "Romayne,"
But to "Mountjoy" later it changed its name.

AOI

L. 3093 *the oriflamme* – the red banner of the Abbey of St-Denis (see note on L. 973); here (incorrectly) identified with the golden banner of the City of Rome.

226

From off his horse the Emperor now descends;
On the green grass he kneels with bended head,
Then to the sunrise he lifts his face addressed
And prays to God with heartfelt reverence:
"Father most true, this day my cause defend!
Thou that to Jonah Thy succour didst extend
In the whale's belly, and safely draw him thence,
And after, spare the King of Nineveh;
Thou that didst save Thy servant Daniel
From torments dire within the lions' den,
And the Three Children amid the fire protect,
Lord, be Thy love this day my present help;
And, if it please Thee, grant that ere this day's end
Roland my nephew may fully be avenged!"
His prayer is done; rising, he stands erect;
The sign of power he makes on brow and breast.
Now to the saddle once more the King has leapt,
Joz'ran and Naimon to hold his stirrup bend;
He takes his shield, his sharpened spear as well;
Comely his body and straight and nobly held,
His face is frank, his looks are confident;
Forward he rides, firm in the stirrup set.
To van, to rear, the braying clarions swell;
Olifant's voice resounds above the rest;
The thought of Roland draws tears from all the French.

227

Right gallantly the Emperor Carlon rides;
Over his byrny he lets his beard float wide;
For love of him the French all do the like:
These hundred thousand may thus be recognised.

They pass the mountains, they pass the rocky heights,
Leave the deep gorges and narrow vales behind;
Forth from the passes and barren lands they hie;
They march across the Spanish country-side,
And in a plain deploy their battle-lines.
To Baligant the scouts return meanwhile,
And one, a Syrian, reports thus what he finds:
"We have seen Carlon, the King, in all his pride.
His men are stubborn, they have no thought of flight.
Arm yourselves now, for you will have to fight."
Quoth Baligant: "That's brave. Have this news cried
To all my Paynims. Go, sound the clarion high!"

228

All through the host they beat the drums of war,
Their trumpets sound, and sound the shrilling horns;
To arm themselves down light the Paynim hordes.
The great Emir is foremost of them all:
He dons a byrny whose skirts are saffron'd o'er,
He's laced his helm with gems and gold adorned,
To his left side he's girded on his sword;
In his great pride he's found a name therefor:
To vie with Carlon's, of which he's heard men talk,
[It bears a title: "Précieuse" the blade is called]
And that's his war-cry when there is battle toward;
To shout this slogan his knights have all been taught
About his neck he hangs his scutcheon broad:
The boss is golden and crystal is the orle,
The strap tough silk with broidered roundels wrought.
Now to his hand his spear Maltet is brought:
The shaft of it is thick as any maul,
The iron alone weighs a mule's load or more.
Now Baligant mounts up upon his horse

(Marcule of Outremer his stirrup caught);
Stalwart is he, capacious in the fork,
Large in the ribs, lean in the flanks and small;
Broad is his breast and beautifully formed,
His shoulders wide, his colour fresh withal,
Warlike his bearing, his curling locks unshorn
White as a flower upon a summer's morn,
His valour proved in battle o'er and o'er;
Were he but Christian, God! what a warrior!
He spurs his steed till the bright blood runs forth,
And goes a-gallop; over a dyke he vaults
Some fifty feet; the Paynims all applaud:
"To keep his marches, lo there a right good lord!
The Frank who seeks to match him force with force
Will he or nill he is riding for a fall.
Carlon's a fool, he ought to have withdrawn!"

AOI

229

A noble sight is the Emir this day:
White is his beard as any flower on spray,
He is in council a man discreet and sage,
And in the battle stubborn and undismayed.
And Malpramis his son's a knight of praise,
Stalwart and tall, a credit to his race.
He tells his father: "Sir, let us ride away!
If we see Carlon I shall be much amazed."
Quoth Baligant: "We shall; for he is brave;
In many a geste he fills an honoured page;
But his great nephew, Roland, is lost and slain;
He has no strength our onslaught to sustain."

AOI

THE SONG OF ROLAND

230

"Lo, Malpramis, fair son," Baligant saith,
"The great lord Roland yesterday met his death,
With Oliver, his brave and noble friend,
And the Twelve Peers, whom Carlon loved the best,
And twenty thousand picked fighters of the French;
Like an old glove I value all the rest.
The Emperor's coming to meet us with his men –
Such is the tale my scout, the Syrian, tells –
A full great force, arranged in columns ten.
Valiant is he who sounds the horn ahead;
An answering call his comrade's clarion sends;
These two ride first, by these the ranks are led;
Franks fifteen thousand they have to ride with them,
Whom Carlon calls 'his sons' – young knights and fresh.
And after these as many more again.
They will do battle right valiantly and well."
Quoth Malpramis: "Give me the honour then."

AOI

231

"Son Malpramis," Baligant answers free,
"Gladly I grant what you have asked of me.
You shall go first to fight the French in field;
The Persian king Torleu shall with you be,
And Dapamort, a Lycian king is he.
If you can beat these braggarts to their knees
Part of my land I'll give to you in fee,
From Cheriant as far as Val Marchis."
Malpramis answers: "Sir, give you gramercy!"
He comes before him and there the gift receives –
The land which then belonged to King Florie,

L. 3200 *the honour* – (of striking the first blow) – see note L. 866.

And now is his; that land he'll never see;
Ne'er of that fief was he vested nor seised.

232

The great Emir goes riding through the host,
And after him his son, of mighty mould,
King Dapamort and King Torleu also.
In thirty columns their force they soon dispose;
Their knighthood makes a marvellous great show –
The least can reckon full fifty thousand souls.
The first is formed of men from Butentrote;
Myconians next, with huge and hairy polls,
Upon whose backs, all down the spine in rows,
As on wild boars, enormous bristles grow;
The third has men from Nubia and Polose,
The fourth, from Brune and the Slavonian coast,
The fifth of Sorbs and Servians is composed,
Sixth, the Moriscoes and the Armenians go;
The seventh's formed of men from Jericho,
The eighth of Negroes, the ninth, of Grosan folk,
The tenth, of men from strong Balida's hold,
Who are a race of most malignant rogues.
Now the Emir has taken a great oath
Upon Mahound, his miracles and bones:
"King Charles of France is coming, the great dolt!
There will be battle, unless he turns and bolts;
His head no more shall wear its crown of gold."

AOI

233

And after this ten columns more they plan:
The first, right hideous, of men from Canaan,
(Out of Val Fuit their road cross-country ran);

The next, of Turks, the third, of Persians,
The fourth, of Petschenegs and Persic bands,
The fifth, of Avars and with them Solterans,
The sixth, of Ugles and of Ormalians,
The seventh column is all Bulgarians,
The eighth of Broussans, the ninth of Claverans,
The tenth, of men from barren Occian,
Sons of the desert, a wild and godless clan;
You'll ne'er hear tell of such repulsive scamps;
Harder than iron their hide on head and flanks,
So that they scorn or harness or steel cap;
They are in battle extremely fierce and rash.

AOI

234

Ten columns more has the Emir anon:
The first has giants that to Malprise belong,
The second, Huns, the third, Hungarians strong,
The fourth's of men from Baldisa-the-Long,
The fifth, of warriors from the Vale Dolorous,
The sixth is formed from the Marusian throng,
The sev'nth of Lechs and men from Astrimon,
The eighth and ninth from Arguille and Clarbonne,
The tenth made up of Longbeards from the Fronde:
These are a people who have no love of God.
Thus thirty columns the Frankish Geste allots.
Great are the hosts, and loud the trumpets' song;
Valiant for war, the Paynim ranks ride on.

AOI

235

The great Emir is mighty and renowned;
His dragon-standard is borne before his powers,
The flag of Termagant and of Mahound,

And of Apollyon an image fierce and foul;
Ten Canaanites escort them all around,
And as they go they thus proclaim aloud:
"Who seeks protection by all these gods of ours
Let him fall prostrate and offer prayer devout!"
Their heads and faces the Paynims all bow down,
All their bright helms they beat upon the ground.
The French all cry: "You'll die, this day, you hounds!
May ruin seize you and all your works confound!
O Lord our God, keep Carlon safe and sound!
In His great name we'll fight this battle out!"

AOI

236

A prudent man is the Emir, and wise;
He calls his son and the two kings aside:
"Barons, my lords, set forward now and ride.
All of my columns I'd have you lead and guide,
Save three reserves I'd keep, of warriors tried.
Firstly, the Turks, next, the Ormalian knights,
And for the third, the giants of Malprise.
And I myself will lead the Occian tribes
With Charlemayn and with his French to fight.
If Carlon seeks to match his strength with mine
He'll have his head shorn from his trunk outright;
That's all he'll get from me – and so he'll find."

AOI

237

Huge are the hosts, their columns show right brave.
Betwixt the two is neither hill nor vale
Forest nor wood; cover is none to take;
In open country they stand there face to face.
Quoth Baligant: "My Paynims, up, away!

Ride forward now the battle to engage!"
Ambure of Olifern the flag has raised;
And on Précieuse the Paynims call by name.
The French all shout: "Great loss you'll have this day!"
And loudly cry: "Mountjoy! Mountjoy!" again.
The Emperor Charles bids all his trumpets bray,
And Olifant sounds louder still than they.
The Paynims cry: "Charles has a fine array;
Battle we'll have; it will be grim and great."

AOI

238

Large is the plain and widely spread the wold.
Bright shine the helms with jewels set in gold,
The gleaming shields, the byrnies' saffron folds,
The glittering spears from which the pennons float.
The clarions bray with loud and piercing notes,
High sounds the charge from Olifant's clear throat.
Now the Emir bids Canabeus approach,
He is his brother, Floridee is his throne,
To Val Sevrée extends his sovereign hold.
He bids him look where Carlon's columns go;
"Lo, there, the pride of far-famed France behold!
And there among them the Emperor riding bold
In the rear ranks amid those long-beards old;
Over their byrnies they've let their beards outflow,
Which are as white as any driven snow.
With lance and spear these men will strike good blows;
We shall have battle, it will be hard and close,
A fight whose like has never yet been known."
Far as a man a peeled white wand could throw,
King Baligant before his people goes;
And, for a speech, says but one word alone:
"Paynims, come on! I'm off to fight the foe."

He shakes the shaft of his good spear right so,
And against Carlon he turns and points the broach.

AOI

239

King Charlemayn, when the Emir he sees
With dragon, standard, and pennon all complete,
Sees the huge force of Arabs now revealed
Filling the country as far as eye can reach,
Save where the host of Carlon sets its feet,
Then the French King (I say) cries hardily:
"Barons of France, good vassals all are ye!
Many's the battle that you have fought in field.
See now these Paynims – a craven folk and mean,
Their false gods' help not worth a penny piece!
Who cares, my lords, how great their numbers be?
Let him go home who will not ride with me!"
Then with the spurs he touches up his steed,
So that beneath him Tencendur gives four leaps.
The French all say: "Why, there's a king indeed!
We're with you to a man. Ride on, good liege!"

240

Clear was the day, bright shone the sun in heaven,
Goodly the armies, the battle-squadrons many;
And face to face the vanguards both stand ready.
Count Guinemanz and Count Rabel make ready,
They loose the bridles of their swift-running destriers
And spur ahead. The French all charge together;
They go to strike with their sharp spears and heavy.

AOI

THE SONG OF ROLAND

241

The Count Rabel is a full hardy knight.
With his gold rowels he spurs his courser light;
Against Torleu, the Persian king, he rides.
Nor shield nor byrny his onset can abide,
Clean through the body the gilded spear he smites;
On a small bush he hurls him dead outright.
The French all say: "Now God be on our side!
We'll not fail Carlon: Carlon is in the right."

AOI

242

And Guinemanz jousts with a Lycian king;
The flower-bright targe he splits from rim to rim
And all asunder scatters the byrny-rings,
Pennon and all drives through the breast of him,
And smites him dead, let laugh or weep who will.
The French cry out to see so shrewd a hit:
"Barons, strike on," they say, "and make no stint!
Against these villains Charles has the right of it!
God His true judgment thus to our hands commits."

AOI

243

Malpramis sits upon a courser white,
Among the Franks through the mellay he strides,
This way and that he turns and fiercely smites,
Corpse upon corpse he flings them down in piles.
Then Baligant before them all makes cry:
"Long years I've kept and fed you, lords of mine.
See how my son in search of Carlon rides,
And with his arms so many lords defies;
A better vassal I could not wish to find.

With your sharp spears go, aid him in the fight!"
He speaks the word; on surge the Paynim lines;
Fierce is the contest, hard are the strokes they strike.
Now wondrous grim and grievous grows the strife,
Like none before, nor since, nor any time.

AOI

244

Great are the hosts, their squadrons very brave.
Now all the columns on both sides are engaged;
The Paynims fight with marvellous fierce rage.
God! what a number of spearshafts snapped in twain!
What splintered shields and shattered byrny-mail!
You'd see the earth strewn with them everyway;
The small green grass you'd see throughout the plain
[With scarlet blood all sprinkled and besprayed.]
Now to his household cries the Emir amain:
"Barons, strike hard against this Christian race!"
Grim is the battle and obstinately waged;
Before or since was never none so great,
There'll be no truce till night shall end the day.

AOI

245

New the Emir appeals to all his troops:
"Strike, Paynims, strike! that's what you're here to do!
I'll give you women, noble and fair of hue,
Honours and fiefs and lands I'll give to you."
The Paynims answer: "Our service is your due."
So hard their strokes, the lances break in two,
By hundred thousand the swords flash into view.
Grim is the battle and terrible and rude;
He learns what war is who fights that battle through.

AOI

246

The Emperor now appeals to all the French:
"Barons, my lords, I love and trust you well.
So many battles you've fought in my defence,
Subdued such kings, conquered so many realms!
Full well I know that I am in your debt
For all I have, my body, lands and wealth.
Your sons, your heirs, your brothers now revenge
That lately fought at Roncevaux and fell!
Justly, you know, I fight the infidel."
The French make answer: "Sir, that is truly said."
Thronging about him are twenty thousand men
Who with one voice their faith and honour pledge
Never to fail him for torment or for death.
With lance and spear there's none but does his best;
Then they draw sword and show more prowess yet.
Fierce is the battle and marvellous and dread.

                                             AOI

247

And Malpramis cleaves through the field on horseback;
Of those of France he makes a grievous slaughter.
Duke Naimon sees him; fierce are his eyes and haughty,
With utmost valour he drives his way athwart him;
He strikes the shield and splits the topmost quarter,
Pierces the hauberk that is of double cordwain,
Clean through his breast the yellow pennon forces,
And flings him dead amid sev'n hundred corpses.

248

King Canabeus, the great Emir's own brother,
Strikes in the spurs and sets his steed a-running.
He's drawn his sword with crystal-mounted pummel;
On the helm's crest he deals Naimon a buffet
So that one-half breaks with the blow and buckles,
And through five laces the trenchant blade goes cutting.
The cap of mail avails him not a button;
Through to the flesh the coif is shorn asunder,
A great piece falls to earth, for all its toughness.
The fearful blow staggered the Duke and stunned him,
Save by God's aid it would have quite undone him;
But he has gripped the horse's neck and clung there,
Should now the Paynim get a chance to redouble
Dead were the baron before he could recover.
Lo! Charles of France speeds to the warrior's succour.

AOI

249

Naimon the Duke is in most deadly peril;
Swiftly the Paynim heaves up his sword to end him.
Carlon cries, "Villain! you'd better not have meddled!"
With all his valour he hurls himself against him,
Hard on his heart he rams the shield and rends it,
And of his hauberk he smashes through the ventail,
And strikes him dead; the saddle is left empty.

250

King Charlemayn is greatly grieved in mind
Thus to see Naimon wounded before his eyes,
To see the blood on the green grass run bright.
Now in his ear the Emperor softly cries:

"Naimon, fair sir, keep closely at my side.
The miscreant's dead that pressed you hard awhile;
I've run him through and done for him this time."
The Duke makes answer: "Your debtor, sir, am I;
I'll not forget it if I come through alive."
Then close together in love and faith they ride,
With twenty thousand good Frenchmen true and tried,
Who never cease each one to hew and smite.

AOI

251

Now the Emir goes riding through the field;
On Guinemanz the Count he rides at speed;
Against his heart he breaks the silver shield,
Rips up the hauberk with all its banded steel,
'Twixt flank and flank he splits his midriff clean,
And flings him dead from his swift-running steed.
Richard the Old, the lord of Normandy,
He slays, and Lorant and Geboïn, all three.
The Paynims cry: "Précieuse is brave indeed!
Strike, barons, strike! a sure defence have we!"

AOI

252

How brave to see the Arab knights engaged,
The men of Occian, Arguille, and Bascle arrayed!
Thrusting and striking they give their spears full play;
Nor do the French once dream of giving way.
Many and many on either side are slain.
Till vesper-tide the fierce encounters rage,
And heavy losses the Frankish lords sustain,
With worse to come before the day is gained!

AOI

253

Both French and Arabs are fighting with a will.
What spears are shattered! how many lances split!
Whoso had seen those shields smashed all to bits,
Heard the bright hauberks gride as the mail-rings rip,
Heard the harsh spear upon the helmet ring,
Seen all those knights out of the saddle spilled,
And the whole earth with death and death-cries filled,
Might long remember the face of suffering!
This is a battle hard to endure, and grim.
Now the Emir invokes his deities –
Mahound, Apollyon, and Termagant, that is:
"O lords my gods, I've served you well ere this;
Now of fine gold I'll make your images
[If against Carlon you grant me grace to win!"]
When lo! Gemalfin appears, his favourite;
Evil indeed the news he has to bring:
"Baligant, sire, for you the day goes ill;
Your son is lost, you have lost Malpramis!
And Canabeus your brother, too, is killed.
It was two Frenchmen that had the luck of it;
The Emperor's self was one of them, I think –
He's great of stature and bears him like a king,
White is his beard as any flower of spring."
Then the Emir his helmèd brow lets sink,
And all his face is darkened and bedimmed;
It seems to him he'll die of grief forthwith.
Jangleu of Outremer he calls to him.

254

Quoth the Emir: "Come here, Jangleu; be frank.
You are a brave and very prudent man
On whose advice I've long been wont to act.
How do they strike you, the Arabs and the Franks?
Will this day give the vict'ry to our hands?"
And he makes answer: "You are dead, Baligant;
Not all your gods can save you from mishap.
Carlon is stubborn, his troops most valiant;
I never yet saw men so fighting-mad.
But call to aid the lords of Occian,
Your Turks and Giants, Arabs and Africans.
Let come what will, delay not, but attack."

255

The great Emir has let his beard flow forth;
It is as white as any flower on thorn:
He'll not stay hidden for aught that may befal.
Now to his lips a trumpet has he caught
And blows so loud, the Paynims hear the call;
From every side they rush to the assault.
The men of Occian whinny and bray and squall,
Those of Arguille like dogs are yelping all.
They charge the Franks with such outrageous force
They break the press and scatter all abroad.
Beneath this shock sev'n thousand fighters fall.

AOI

256

The Count Ogier was never meek of mood:
Vassal more staunch the byrny ne'er endued.
When he beheld the French ranks broken through

He called on Thierry, that of Argonne was duke,
Count Jozeran, and Geoffrey of Anjou,
And Carlon's self he sternly thus rebukes:
"See how the Paynims make havoc of your troops!
God smite the crown from off the head of you
If for this shame you take not vengeance due!"
There's none replies one word to this reproof;
They spur their steeds, they let the bridles loose,
And ride to strike them where'er there's most to do.

AOI

257

Right bravely fights King Charlemayn this day,
Brave is Duke Naimon, brave is Ogier the Dane.
Geoffrey, who bears the gonfalon, is brave;
Bravest of all is Dan Ogier the Dane.
He spurs his horse and lets him run apace,
The dragon-bearer with furious force assails
And sends him crashing; down goes Ambure full weight,
Dragon and ensign and all, upon the plain,
Baligant sees his pennon cast away,
Sees Mahound's banner brought to a sudden stay;
Then the Emir begins to be afraid
The wrong's with him, the right with Charlemayn.
The Arab Paynims falter amid the fray.
The Emperor's voice rings out: "To aid! to aid!
Will you not help me, lords barons, o'God's name!"
The Franks reply: "Why ask? You do us shame –
Cursèd be he that will not strike amain!"

AOI

258

The day draws on, twilight begins to lower;
Paynim and Frank are now at swords throughout.
Valiant are they that have disposed the powers,
Neither forget they their battle-cries to shout;
From the Emir the call "Précieuse!" resounds,
Charles shouts "Mountjoy!" his battle-cry renowned;
They know each other by these clear calls and loud,
Each in mid-field has sought his foe and found.
They meet, they charge, exchanging mighty clouts,
On the ringed shields crash home the spearheads stout;
Clean from the bosses they break them all about,
They rend the hauberks, the mail-rings fall in showers,
But both their bodies are left untouched and sound,
The girths are burst, the saddles swivel round,
They fall to earth, and both the kings are down!
But to his feet each of them lightly bounds.
Great is their valour; at once their swords are out.
Nothing at all can part this combat now;
It will not cease till one lies dead on ground.

                                        AOI

259

Charles of fair France is a great man of might,
And the Emir knows naught of fear or flight.
Their naked swords they brandish now on high,
Lay on the shields stiff strokes from either side,
Shearing the leather and wood of double ply;
The rivets fall, in shreds the buckles fly.
In their bare byrnies now breast to breast they fight,
The glittering sparks flash from the helmets bright.
Nothing at all can ever end their strife
Till one confess he's wrong, the other right.

                                        AOI

260

Quoth the Emir: "Bethink thee, Charles, and see
That thou repent what thou hast done to me.
My son is slain; I know it was by thee;
And on my lands thou wrongfully hast seized.
Become my man, and I will be thy liege;
Then come and serve me from here unto the East."
Quoth Carlon: "Nay, I'd hold it treachery;
Never to Paynims may I show love or peace.
Do thou confess the Faith by God revealed,
Take Christendom, and thy fast friend I'll be.
The King Almighty then serve thou and believe."
Quoth Baligant: "Thy sermon's but ill preached."
Once more with swords they battle, each to each.

AOI

261

The great Emir is full of power and skill;
On Carlon's helm he lays a mighty hit,
That on his head the steel is rent and split;
Downward the blade through hair and scalp he brings
And of the flesh shears off a whole palm's width,
So that the bone shows bare beneath the skin.
King Carlon reels and well-nigh falls with it.
But God wills not he be o'ercome or killed;
Saint Gabriel comes hastening down to him:
"And what," saith he, "art thou about, great King?"

262

When Charles thus hears the blessed Angel say,
He fears not death, he's free from all dismay,
His strength returns, he is himself again.

At the Emir he drives his good French blade,
He carves the helm with jewel-stones ablaze,
He splits the skull, he dashes out the brains,
Down to the beard he cleaves him through the face,
And, past all healing, he flings him down, clean slain.
His rallying-cry, "Mountjoy!", he shouts straightway.
At this, Duke Naimon comes, leading by the rein
Good Tenecendur, and up mounts Charlemayn.
The Paynims fly, God will not have them stay.
All's done, all's won; the French have gained the day.

263

The Paynims fly, for God has willed it so.
Hard in pursuit see Franks and Emperor go!
Then saith the King: "My lords, avenge your woes;
Work all your will, lift up your hearts and souls,
For, but this morning, I saw your eyes o'erflow."
"Sir," say the Franks, "indeed it so behoves."
With all their might they deal tremendous blows;
Of those who're there few will escape their strokes.

264

Fierce is the heat, the dust goes up in clouds.
The Paynims flee, the French behind them scour,
The chase endures to Saragossa town.
Queen Bramimonda mounts up into her tower;
Beside her stand her clerks and canons vowed
To that false faith which God has disallowed –
Priests without orders, no tonsures on their crowns.
Seeing the Arabs thus beaten all about,
In a shrill voice she cries: "To help, Mahound!
Ah, noble King! our men are put to rout!
The great Emir is killed! O shameful hour!"

When this he hears, Marsilion turns him round
Face to the wall; he weeps, he droops his brow,
He dies of grief, by direful doom struck down,
And yields his soul to the infernal powers.

AOI

265

The Paynims all are dead or fled in terror,
And Carlon's war is gloriously ended.
He lays the gate of Saragossa level;
Right well he knows it will not be defended.
He takes the city and with his army enters;
That night they lie there, as victors in possession;
Proudly he goes, the silver-bearded Emperor.
All of her towers Queen Bramimond surrenders –
Her ten tall towers and fifty that are lesser.
Well speeds that man which hath God for his helper.

266

The day is past, the dark draws on to night,
Clear is the moon, the stars are shining bright;
All Saragossa lies in the Emperor's might.
Some thousand French search the whole town, to spy
Synagogues out and mosques and heathen shrines.
With heavy hammers and with mallets of iron
They smash the idols, the images they smite,
Make a clean sweep of mummeries and lies,
For Charles fears God and still to serve Him strives.
The Bishops next the water sanctify;
Then to the font the Paynim folk they drive.
Should Carlon's orders by any be defied
The man is hanged or slain or burned with fire.

L. 3670 *hanged* – reading, with Whitehead "pendre"; the MS has *prendre* (taken).

An hundred thousand or more are thus baptized
And christened, – only the Queen fares otherwise:
She's to go captive to fair France by and by,
Her would the King convert by love to Christ.

267

The night is past, up rises the clear day.
Of Saragossa Charles mans the towers straightway;
Stout knights a thousand the Emperor designates
On his behalf to keep the city safe.
Then King and army get them to horse again,
With Bramimond a captive in their train;
Nought but her good seeks Charles, her soul to save.
With joy and triumph the homeward road they take.
They storm Narbonne and leave it by the way,
And reach Bordeaux, a city of great fame.
There, on the altar of Sev'rin the good saint,
Filled with gold mangons, the Olifant they lay,
(Pilgrims may see it when visiting the place)
And cross Gironde, where much good shipping waits.
So the King brings his nephew back to Blaye,
With his companion, Count Oliver the great,
And the Archbishop, that was so wise and brave.
All in white tombs these noble men are laid:
There lie they still, good lords, in St Romayne's;
The French commend them to God, His power and Name
Carlon rides on, up mountain and down vale,
Making no stay until he comes to Aix,
And lights at length before the palace gates.
When he has set him in his high hall of state
To call his judges he sends out writs in haste:
Saxons, Bavarians, and Frisians and Lorrains,
Burgundians too he calls; men of Almayne

And Normandy and Poitou and Bretayne,
And those of France, learn'd above all and sage;
Ganelon now must stand to be arraigned.

268

Homeward from Spain the Emperor Charles has sped
And come to Aix, France's best citadel.
Into his hall he climbs the palace steps;
There comes to meet him Aude, a fair damozel.
She asks the King: "Where is the captain dread?
Say, where is Roland that promised me to wed?"
Then Carlon's heart is filled with heaviness,
His eyes weep tears, his snowy beard he rends:
"Sister, sweet lady, you ask me for the dead.
A man yet nobler I'll give to you instead:
Louis, I mean – what better can I else?
He is my son, and heir to all my realm."
"To me," saith Aude, "these words are meaningless.
God and His saints and angels now forfend
I should live on when Roland's life is spent!"
At Carlon's feet she falls, her hue is fled,
She dies forthwith, God give her spirit rest!
The French lords weep and grievously lament.

269

Aude the Fair has made an end of life.
The King thinks only that she has swooned outright.
He pities her, the tears fall from his eyes;
He takes her hands, he seeks to bid her rise,
But on her shoulders her drooping head declines.
When Carlon sees that she indeed has died,
Four countesses he summons to her side;

Unto a convent of nuns she's borne to lie.
Till the day breaks they watch by her all night,
Then, near an altar, she's tombed with solemn rites.
Charles does her honour as much as in him lies.

AOI

270

The Emperor Charles to Aix is now come back;
Now Ganelon the false, in iron bands,
Amid the city before the palace stands.
Unto a stake the varlets have him strapped,
With deer-hide thongs they have fettered his hands,
With rods and cudgels they give him many a thwack:
No other guerdon has he deserved but that.
He waits for judgment, with pain and anguish racked.

271

In the old Geste 'tis writ for all to read
How Carlon summons vassals from all his fiefs.
Now in the city, Aix-la-Chapelle, they meet.
It is a high-day, a very solemn feast –
St Sylvester, so many men agree.
Now we begin the judgment and the plea
Of Ganelon who did the treacherous deed.
The Emperor bids them hale him before his seat.

AOI

272

"Barons, my lords," then saith King Charlemayn,
"Judge you 'twixt me and Ganelon this day.
He went with me and with my host to Spain;
By twenty thousand he's had my Frenchmen slain,
Also my nephew, whom you'll not see again,

And Oliver, that courteous lord and brave –
All the Twelve Peers for money he betrayed."
"I'd scorn," quoth Guènes, "not to admit that same;
Roland had wronged me in wealth and in estate,
Therefore I plotted his death and his disgrace.
But I deny treason against the state."
The Franks reply: "This calls for much debate."

273

Before the King stood forth Count Ganelon;
Comely his body and fresh his colour was;
A man right noble he'd seem, were he not false.
He eyes the French, his judges all he cons,
And his supporters, thirty of his own stock;
Then cries aloud in a clear voice and strong:
"Hear me, my lords, now for the love of God!
Sirs, with the army indeed I went along,
In faith and love I served the Emperor long.
Roland his nephew hated and did me wrong –
Doomed me to die, horribly, by a plot.
I was made envoy to King Marsilion,
But used my wits, and so came safely off.
I defied Roland, that fighting fanfaron,
And Oliver, and all their champions.
Charles and his barons heard me, as well they wot.
Vengeance I took, but treason did I not."
The Franks reply: "We must debate thereof."

274

When Guènes sees his judgment thus begin
He has about him thirty of his own kin;
There's one to whom the rest yield leadership,

Called Pinabel; Sorence his castle is.
He's a good speaker and nimble of his wit,
And to bear arms he is both strong and skilled.
Quoth Ganelon: "See me not shamed or killed!
I trust you, friend, to get me out of this."
Quoth Pinabel: "And get you out I will,
If any Frenchman should sentence you to swing,
Carlon must set us face to face in the lists;
With my bright brand I'll give the lie to him!"
Count Guènes bows, his very feet to kiss.

275

Saxons, Bavarians, to council now retreat
With those of France, Poitou, and Normandy,
And many Teutons and men of Germany –
Those of Auvergne use the most courtesy.
Softly, for fear of Pinabel, they speak:
"This trial," say they, "'twere best to let it be.
Abandon it, and to the King make plea
That for this once Ganelon should go free,
And after serve him in faith and loyalty.
Roland is dead – he'll never more be seen –
One can't restore him for money or for fee.
Fight Pinabel? Who'd be so rash? Not me!"
One and one only refuses to agree:
Lord Geoffrey's brother, that is by name Thierry.

AOI

276

To Charlemayn these lords return once more;
They tell the King: "Thus humbly prays your court:
That you should pardon Count Ganelon his fault,
And he will serve you in faith and love henceforth.

Pray let him live; he is right nobly born;
His death can never bring back that valiant lord,
Nor yet for money can the dead be restored."
The King replies: "False traitors are ye all."

AOI

277

When Carlon finds them all failing him and shirking,
His brow grows dark, his countenance is burdened
With grief to see a cowardice so scurvy.
When lo! a knight, Thierry, is up and stirring –
Brother to Geoffrey Duke of Anjou, by birthright;
He's lean of body, his limbs are lithe and nervous,
His skin is swarthy and his hair black and curling,
Not very tall nor very short you'd term him.
Thus to the Emperor he speaks in manner courteous:
"Fair Lord and King, let not these griefs perturb you.
You know full well how faithfully I've served you,
This quarrel's mine, by right of race and nurture.
Even if Roland did Guènes some disservice,
Your officers are sacred in their persons,
And to betray him was treachery and murder;
It was to you, sir, Guènes was false and perjured.
I sentence him to death by hanging – further
To have his body [dragged meanly on a hurdle,]
As well befits such treasonable vermin.
Should any kinsman of his dispute my verdict,
Then, with the sword that hangs here at my girdle,
At any moment I'm ready to confirm it."
The Franks all cry: "Well have you said, for certain!"

278

Pinabel now before the King has come;
He's strong and agile and very big and tough:
Where his blow lands, the sands of life are run.
He says to Carlon: "Is this your court, sir? Tush!
Tell all those people to stop this noise at once.
Here I see Thierry, who sets up for a judge.
He lies. I'll fight him: his throat shall take the thrust."
He gives the King his right-hand deerskin glove.
The King says: "Find me good hostages enough."
The thirty kinsmen pledge him, by faith and trust.
"I," says the Emperor, "will pledge the other one."
He has them guarded till justice shall be done.

                                        AOI

279

When Thierry sees the combat will be waged,
He gives to Carlon his right-hand glove as gage.
In pledge for him the Emperor plights his faith,
Then bids them bring four benches to the place;
The combatants sit down on these and wait.
Everyone thinks this challenge well arranged;
Procedure's settled by Lord Ogier the Dane.
This done, they call for horse and arms straightway.

                                        AOI

LL. 3845 sqq. These lines describe the regular etiquette of the ordeal by
battle: the challenger offers his gauntlet as battle-gage, and the champion
of the accused offers his, in token of his acceptance of the challenge. Sureties
are demanded on either side to go bail for their principal's appearance. The
lists are set up, with four benches (L. 3853) for the combatants (and their
sureties) to sit upon, and an officer (L. 3856) is appointed to supervise the
proceedings. On the appointed day, the combatants attend Mass and receive
Communion (L. 3859) before presenting themselves for the combat.

280

When for the combat they are prepared and dight
They make confession and are absolved and signed,
And so hear mass and eat the bread of Christ,
And to the churches vow off'rings of great price.
Then they return to Carlon, side by side,
Upon their heels their spurs are buckled tight,
They've donned their hauberks, subtle and strong and white,
Laced to their heads their glittering helmets bright,
Girt on their swords with pure gold hilts made fine;
About their necks their quartered scutcheons shine;
In their right hands the pointed spears they gripe.
Then up they mount upon their coursers light.
Men weep to see them, full hundred thousand knights,
Who grieve for Roland and pity Thierry's plight.
God alone knows which way will end the fight.

AOI

281

Beneath Aix walls an ample plain extends,
Here, face to face, the combatants are set.
Both are right noble, in valour they excel,
Spirited steeds they have, that run full well.
They spur them hard, loose rein upon their necks,
Right gallantly they ride to strike – they've met!
Mid-shield they strike, the bucklers break and bend,
The hauberks split, the saddle-girths are rent,
Twisting to earth go saddle-bow and selle –
They weep to see them, those hundred thousand men.

AOI

L. 3881 *selle* – saddle

282

Down to the ground they've fallen, both the fighters.
But to their feet at once they leap up lightly;
Pinabel's strong and very swift and sprightly;
Their steeds are gone – each runs to meet his rival.
Now with their swords whose hilts are gilded brightly
On the steel helmets they're buffeting and striking –
Heavy their strokes, great fragments are sent flying.
The French well-nigh go crazy with excitement.
"Ah, God!" cries Carlon, "declare Thou where the right is."

283

Quoth Pinabel: "Thierry, I charge thee yield!
By love and faith thy vassal I will be,
Whate'er thou wilt I'll give of gold and fee,
Only 'twixt Carlon and Ganelon make peace!"
Thierry replies: "This needs no thought from me.
Right base were I the least thing to concede.
May God do justice this day 'twixt me and thee!"

AOI

284

Then Thierry saith: "Pinabel, thou art brave,
Sturdy and strong, thy limbs are nobly framed;
Thy peers know well thy valour is unstained:
I do beseech thee, quit now, and yield the day!
Gladly I'll make thy peace with Charlemayn;
To Ganelon, such justice shall be weighed
That till time end the world shall tell the tale."
Pinabel answers: "Forbid it God, I say!
I will uphold the honour of my race;
There's no man living shall ever see me quail;

I'd rather die than so be put to shame."
Then with their swords they start to strike again
Upon their helms with gold and jewels gay;
Sky-high the sparks fly in a fiery spray.
They'll not be parted; their fury none can stay;
Till one lie dead nothing can end the fray.

AOI

285

Pinabel's strong, the valiant Sorence knight.
On Thierry's helm of Provence steel he smites;
The flash leaps out and sets the grass a-fire.
Then with the point at Thierry's face he drives,
And on his forehead delivers such a swipe
That from his face [the blade carves off a slice,]
Leaving his cheek all bloodied on the right,
The hauberk streaming, both back and breast alike.
But for God's help, that stroke had cost his life.

AOI

286

When Thierry feels the blade bite through his flesh,
And sees the blood upon the grass run red,
Then he lets drive a blow at Pinabel.
Down to the nasal he cleaves the bright steel helm,
Shears through the brain and spills it from his head,
Wrenches the blade out and shakes him from it dead.
With that great stroke he wins and makes an end.
The Franks all cry: "God's might is manifest!
Justice demands the rope for Guènes's neck,
And for his kinsmen who set their lives in pledge!"

AOI

287

Now Thierry's battle triumphantly is ended,
Straight to his side comes Charlemayn the Emperor;
Four of his barons are with him in attendance:
The good Duke Naimon, the Lord Ogier of Denmark,
William of Blaye, and the Angevin, Geoffrey.
In his two arms the King embraces Thierry,
With his rich sables his countenance he cleanses;
Then lays these by, and in others they dress him.
Next they disarm the champion very gently,
And on a mule of Araby they set him.
So they return, joyous and making merry,
And come to Aix, in the great square descending;
Then for those others they prepare the death-sentence.

AOI

288

Carlon now summons all his counts and his dukes:
"How do you rede me these hostages to use?
They came to second Ganelon in this suit,
And pledged themselves for Pinabel to boot."
The Franks reply: "Spare none; death is their due."
Then the King orders an officer, Basbrun:
"Go, hang them all upon the tree of doom.
By this my beard that silver is of hue,
If one escapes there's death and dole for you!"
The man replies: "And what else should I do?"
A hundred sergeants hale away the whole crew;
Each of the thirty is hanged up in a noose.
Treason destroys itself and others too.

AOI

l. 3951 *death is their due* – the wholesale slaughter of the vanquished man's
sureties is not the ordinary mediaeval practice. Presumably, in this case,
they are held to have abetted Ganelon's treason.

289

Now the Bavarians, the men of Germany
And Brittany, Poitou and Normandy,
But first, the French, are then and there agreed;
Ganelon's death by torture is decreed.
So to this end they order up four steeds,
And bind him to them by the hands and the feet.
High-mettled stallions they are, exceeding fleet;
Four sergeants take them and urge them at full speed
Towards a mare running loose in a field.
Ganelon's torment is fearful and extreme,
For all his sinews are racked from head to heel,
His every limb wrenched from the sockets clean;
His blood runs bright upon the grassy green.
Ganelon's dead – so perish all his breed!
'Twere wrong that treason should live to boast the deed.

290

The Emperor's debt of vengeance now is paid;
Next, his French bishops he summons to his aid,
Bavarian bishops, and bishops of Almayn:
"Lodged captive here I have a noble dame.
Sermon and story on her heart have prevailed
God to believe and Christendom to take;
Therefore baptize her that her soul may be saved."
"Provide her then with godmothers," they say,
["Nobly-born ladies, instructed in the Faith."]
Great the assembly about the Baths at Aix;
There they baptize Bramimond, Queen of Spain,

L. 3968 *mare* – reading with Léon Gautier ewe < equa; other editors read ewe < aqua and render "water". The mare seems to give the more vivid picture, though the other rendering has rather more critical support.

And Juliana they've chosen for her name;
Christian is she, informed in the True Way.

291

The Emperor now has ended his assize
With justice done, his great wrath satisfied,
And Bramimonda brought to the fold of Christ.
The day departs and evening turns to night;
The King's abed in vaulted chamber high;
St Gabriel comes, God's courier, to his side:
"Up, Charles! assemble thy whole imperial might;
With force and arms unto Elbira ride;
Needs must thou succour King Vivien where he lies
At Imphe, his city, besieged by Paynim tribes;
There for thy help the Christians call and cry."
Small heart had Carlon to journey and to fight;
"God!" says the King, "how weary is my life!"
He weeps, he plucks his flowing beard and white.

Here ends the geste Turoldus would recite.

A vostre femme enveierai dous nusches . . .
Il les ad prises, en sa hoese les butet.

This pair of owches on your wife I bestow . . .
He takes the jewels and thrusts them in his poke.

These lines present certain problems both to the linguist and to the student of period costume.

To begin with, what exactly is a "nusche" (owch)? The dictionary offers (1) collar, (2) bracelet, (3) brooch. The first meaning is unlikely in the context: the reference seems to be to something which goes in pairs. Either "bracelets" or "brooches" would thus fill the bill, but Dr Joan Evans is of the opinion that the word is seldom or never applied to an *annular* object. It therefore seems probable that Bramimonda's gift was a pair of *brooches*, such as would be used for fastening a cloak below the throat.

Having received the jewels, Ganelon proceeds to thrust them into his *hoese*. The word (from the Germanic *hosa*) is usually translated "boot"; but since the foot-gear of the period is very ill-adapted for the transport of stiff and bulky pieces of jewellery, this rendering appears to offer practical difficulties.

The alternatives that have been suggested to me are:

(1) *hose*. This appears attractive; but the usual French equivalent of the English "hose" is "chauce" (the modern "chausse"). Moreover, there does not seem to be any clear evidence that the long hose of the period (the legs tailored separately from cloth cut on the cross, and attached to the waist by points) were provided with pockets. It is true that Vivian in the *Chançun de Willame* does produce a pennon from his *chauces*; but this, being soft, could have been tucked in at the top; "owches" would make an unsightly bulge, and would (one feels) be apt to "work down" disconcertingly.

(2) It is conceivable that the scribe may have accidentally written hoese< hosa for huece< hulcia = *cloak*, since the two words were almost identically pronounced. In that case, if the "nusches" were brooches, Ganelon would simply have thrust them into his cloak

by the pins. But philologists are rightly reluctant to postulate scribal errors *praeter necessitatem*.

(3) What one would naturally expect Ganelon to use for stowing parcels is the *pouch* in which every gentleman of the period carried his money and other small movables, and which was worn attached to a belt, either above or below his outer garment. It is not easy to find unambiguous examples of the use of *hoese* in this sense, nor yet of the cognate Italian *uosa* (deriving likewise from Ger. *hosa*). I am, however, indebted to Dr Barbara Reynolds for the information that the latter word has a diminutive, *usatto*, which appears to have meant pouch as well as boot. The context here is happily quite unambiguous. In the thirteenth century *Vita di S. Domenico*, a boy suffering from hernia is described as having gone about for the space of two years with his innards enclosed in an *usatto*. Whatever may have been done with owches, dragon's claws and other such trifles as the heroes of geste and romance from time to time bestowed about their persons, the unfortunate child with the hernia cannot possibly have put his bowels in his boots – or even in his cloak or his hose. Consequently we may reasonably argue that if *usatto* meant "pouch" then *hoese* may have had the same meaning, which is the one that best fits the *Roland* context. Moreover, in a sixteenth century prescription for the cure of jealousy we find the word "heuse" used, in exactly the same way as "minot", to mean a measure or container:

> "Prenez de soucy plaine heuse
> Et de pensées plain un minot".

Compare the English use, "a pocket (small sack) of hops"; "a pocket full of rye." I have accordingly rendered the word "poke" somewhat tentatively, but still trusting that this is a reasonable possibility, and not mere wishful thinking. (It will be noticed that the Eng. *poke*, *pouch*, and the Fr. *poche*, *pochette*, stand in much the same relation to one another as the group Fr. *hoese*, It. *uosa*, *usatto*.)

LINCOLN CHRISTIAN UNIVERSITY

FOR THE BEST IN PAPERBACKS, LOOK FOR THE (

In every corner of the world, on every subject under the sun, Penguin represe quality and variety—the very best in publishing today.

For complete information about books available from Penguin—includ Penguin Classics, Penguin Compass, and Puffins—and how to order them, w to us at the appropriate address below. Please note that for copyright reasons selection of books varies from country to country.

In the United States: Please write to *Penguin Group (USA), P.O. Box 12. Dept. B, Newark, New Jersey 07101-5289* or call 1-800-788-6262.

In the United Kingdom: Please write to *Dept. EP, Penguin Books Ltd, I Road, Harmondsworth, West Drayton, Middlesex UB7 0DA.*

In Canada: Please write to *Penguin Books Canada Ltd, 90 Eglinton Avenue E Suite 700, Toronto, Ontario M4P 2Y3.*

In Australia: Please write to *Penguin Books Australia Ltd, P.O. Box 2 Ringwood, Victoria 3134.*

In New Zealand: Please write to *Penguin Books (NZ) Ltd, Private Bag 1029 North Shore Mail Centre, Auckland 10.*

In India: Please write to *Penguin Books India Pvt Ltd, 11 Panchsheel Shop Centre, Panchsheel Park, New Delhi 110 017.*

In the Netherlands: Please write to *Penguin Books Netherlands bv, Postbus 35 NL-1001 AH Amsterdam.*

In Germany: Please write to *Penguin Books Deutschland GmbH, Metzlerstr 26, 60594 Frankfurt am Main.*

In Spain: Please write to *Penguin Books S. A., Bravo Murillo 19, 1° B, 28 Madrid.*

In Italy: Please write to *Penguin Italia s.r.l., Via Benedetto Croce 2, 20094 Co Milano.*

In France: Please write to *Penguin France, Le Carré Wilson, 62 rue Benja Baillaud, 31500 Toulouse.*

In Japan: Please write to *Penguin Books Japan Ltd, Kaneko Building, 2-3 Koraku, Bunkyo-Ku, Tokyo 112.*

In South Africa: Please write to *Penguin Books South Africa (Pty) Ltd, Private X14, Parkview, 2122 Johannesburg.*

8491016

841.1
C458
1957

LINCOLN CHRISTIAN UNIVERSITY

12423

3 4711 00208 5498

LINCOLN CHRISTIAN COLLEGE & SEMINARY